# TREASURY OF
# DOLLS &
# CUDDLY TOYS

# TREASURY OF
# DOLLS &
# CUDDLY TOYS

**MURDOCH BOOKS**®
*Sydney • London • Vancouver • New York*

**Dolls** in the form of girls, boys
and adults, and toys made to resemble favourite animals
have existed for thousands of years in every civilisation.
Play and make-believe have always been part of childhood and
growing-up. This collection of lovable dolls and soft toys to sew,
knit and crochet, from the craft editors of Family Circle is designed
to give you, your children and young friends lots of fun.

On the following pages are complete instructions and diagrams
for dolls and cuddly soft toys, ranging from life-size to tiny.

Mostly made from scraps of fabric and yarn, they give you
the ultimate in cleverly designed, safe playthings at minimum cost.

What's more, you will enjoy making them to give for birthdays,
Christmas — or simply for love.

JOY HAYES

# CONTENTS

## List of Abbreviations

### Knitting

K—*Knit*; P—*Purl*; st(s)—*stitch(es)*; cont—*continue*; tog—*together*; st st—*stocking stitch*; inc—*increase*; dec—*decrease*; rep—*repeat*; alt—*alternate*; foll—*following*; rem—*remaining*; beg—*beginning*; patt—*pattern*; yfwd—*yarn forward*; pmon—*place marker on needle*; sl st—*slip stitch*; psso—*pass slip stitch over*; ybk—*yarn back*; make 1—*pick up loop between sts on left hand needle and knit into back of loop*.

### Crochet

ch—*chain*; sc—*single crochet*; dc—*double crochet*; tr—*treble*; rnd(s)—*round(s)*; inc—*increase*; dec—*decrease*; rep—*repeat*; alt—*alternate*; foll—*following*; rem—*remaining*; beg—*beginning*; patt—*pattern*; lp st(s)—*loop stitch(es)*.

## How to Enlarge Patterns

Draw crisscross lines, vertically and horizontally, with a ruler, on brown wrapping paper, spacing the lines as indicated. Then copy our pattern, one square at a time, using ruler or compass. Cut out enlarged pattern and use as directed in instructions.

## Stitches

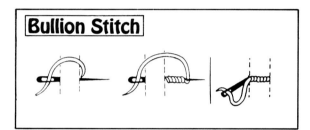

**Bullion Stitch**

**Trammed Gros Point Stitch**

(a) Work a trammed stitch from left to right, then pull the needle through on the lower line; insert the needle diagonally into the upper line crossing the laid thread and one intersection of canvas threads (the point where a pair of narrow vertical threads cross a pair of narrow horizontal threads); bring the needle through on the lower line two canvas thread intersections to the left. Continue in this way to the end of the row.

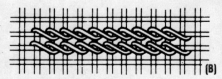

(b) Shows the reverse side of correctly worked gros point stitch where the length of the stitches is greater than those on the correct side.

## Pompon

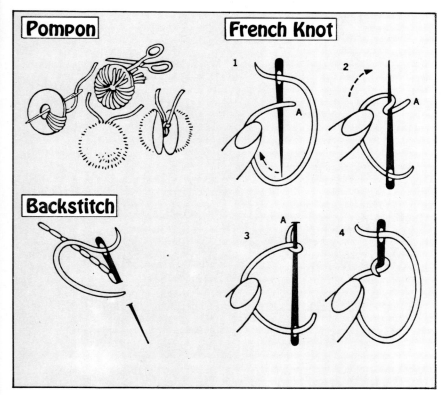

## French Knot

## Backstitch

## Lazy Daisy Stitch

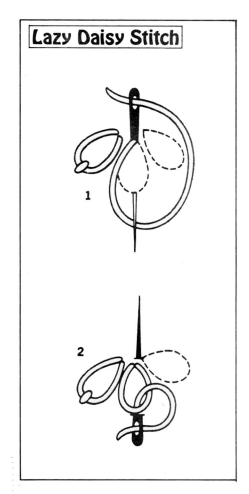

## Loop Stitch

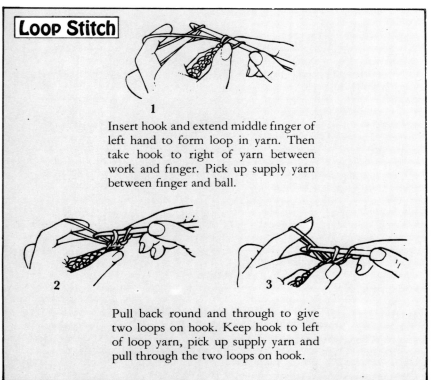

**1**

Insert hook and extend middle finger of left hand to form loop in yarn. Then take hook to right of yarn between work and finger. Pick up supply yarn between finger and ball.

**2**        **3**

Pull back round and through to give two loops on hook. Keep hook to left of loop yarn, pick up supply yarn and pull through the two loops on hook.

7

# My Baby Doll

DESIGNED BY GWEN MERRILL

Just like a real baby, this doll has its own carry-basket and liner, mattress, pillow and quilt, plus a layette consisting of a knitted vest and booties, flannel pilchers, nappy and nightie. For daytime, a knitted angel top, leggings, and an old-world dress and bonnet.

To make patterns, enlarge doll and clothing patterns (see Figs 1–3), working to a scale 1 sq = 2.5 cm. A 5 mm seam allowance is included on all pattern pieces. Sew all seams with right sides together unless otherwise indicated. See pp. 14–17 for patterns.

*Note:* For body, sew all seams twice and trim only where necessary.

*Abbreviations:* K — *Knit*; P — *Purl*; st(s) — *stitch(es)*; cont — *continue*; tog — *together*; st st — *stocking stitch*; inc — *increase*; dec — *decrease*; yfwd — *yarn forward*; pmon — *place marker on needle*; sl st — *slip stitch*; dc — *double crochet*; ch — *chain*; tr — *treble*; rep — *repeat*; alt — *alternate*; foll — *following*; beg — *beginning*; patt — *pattern*.

## BABY DOLL
### (height 48 cm)

50 × 90 cm wide calico
scraps of brown, black, pink and beige felt for face
approximately 10 m thick (at least 20-ply) bouclé wool for hair
1 pr 6.50 mm (No. 3) knitting needles
polyester fibre for filling
fabric glue

### To make body

1. Cut two body pieces, four arms, four legs, two soles, two front side head, two back side head, one head gusset and four ears.
2. Sew ears and trim seam, turn to right side and fill loosely. Baste across opening. Sew each to right side of side back head pieces, with raw edges together. Sew side back head to side front head at edges (A). Make dart for chin on wrong side of head gusset. Sew gusset to side head pieces from front to back neck on both sides. Turn to right side.

*My Baby Doll in dress and bonnet*

3. Sew arms and nick curves, turn to right side and fill loosely. Sew across raw edges. Pleat arms to fit and sew to right side of back body at armholes between dots. Fold front body on to back, covering arm and sew from neck across arm to make dart.
4. Sew body pieces together at centre front and back. Insert head inside body, matching chin dart with centre front seam and sew around several times. Turn to right side. Fold 5 mm seam allowance to wrong side around lower body and baste. Fill head and neck firmly, using small pieces to define the cheeks and chin. Fill body loosely.
5. Sew front and back leg seams, clip curves. Nick seam allowance of foot before sewing to soles. Trim seam and turn to right side. Fill leg to within 2 cm of top, sew across opening with seams in the centre. Insert legs in body and handsew around firmly on both sides.
6. Cut eyes, cheeks and mouth in felt and glue to face.

### To make hair

Use bouclé wool and 6.50 mm knitting needles.
Cast on 12 sts. Knit 6 rows, slip the first st of every row.
*7th row:* Slip 1, K2, inc 1, K to last 4 sts, inc 1, K3.
*8th row:* Slip first st, K to end of row.
Rep these 2 rows until 24 sts.
Work extra rows on 24 sts if this is not enough hair.
*Next row:* K2 tog, K2, K2 tog, K to last 6 sts, K2 tog, K2, K2 tog (20 sts).
*Next row:* Slip first st, K to end of row.
Rep these 2 rows until 12 sts rem.
*Next row:* K2 tog, K2, K2 tog twice, K2, K2 tog (8 sts).
*Next row:* Slip first st, K to end of row.
*Next row:* Dec first and last st (6 sts).
Cast off.

### To attach hair

Pin cast-on edge of hair across back of head approximately 2 cm from neck seam. Pin row ends around back of ear with widest section of knitting ending in front of ear. Shape remaining edge to form a peak at forehead. Handsew securely to head.

## PILCHERS AND NAPPY

26 × 48 cm wide piece flannel or suitable substitute
four 12 mm buttons
32 cm square of towelling
safety pin

### Pilchers

1. Make pattern (*see Fig. 2*).
2. Cut two pilcher pieces and sew around twice leaving an opening at centre back. Clip curves and corners. Turn to right side and press. Handsew across opening. Topstitch around 5 mm from edge on right side. Work four buttonholes on front. Sew on buttons.

### Nappy

Turn in raw edges and zigzag around. Fold into a triangle and pin on baby.

## NIGHTIE

60 × 90 cm wide fine white cotton
four 10 mm buttons
shirring elastic
75 cm lace edging
two colours stranded embroidery thread for rosebuds

1. Make pattern (*see Fig. 2*).
2. Cut one front, two backs and two sleeves.
3. Sew sleeves to front and backs at armholes. Neaten seams and press. To zigzag around raw edge of neck and bottom of sleeves, adjust stitch length to small and width to widest setting. Practise on a scrap of material first to achieve a firm corded edge and check that stitching will not pull away from fabric.
4. Press back facing to wrong side. Thread bobbin with shirring elastic. Adjust stitch length to largest stitch. Practise on a scrap of material to achieve correct tension and amount of gathering. With garment flat, begin shirring at centre back 2 cm from folded facing edge. Stitch around to other side, keeping edge of foot parallel

to neatened edge. Work four more rows in the same way. Keep rows the same distance apart and make sure that fabric is kept flat for outer rows.

*Note:* If the first row is too loose, unpick shirring and work another row without pulling fabric quite flat. Work one row shirring around hems of sleeves in same way. Tie all ends securely.

5. Sew and neaten underarm and side seams. Press and sew lace to nightie hem, neaten seam. Work four buttonholes at back, sew on buttons. Embroider rosebuds around yoke, following directions given for booties.

## DRESS AND BONNET

50 × 90 cm wide printed cotton
20 × 48 cm wide piece plain cotton for yoke
28 × 32 cm wide piece plain cotton for bonnet crown
1.7 m of lace edging
1.2 m of 5 mm wide ribbon
three 12 mm buttons
two colours stranded embroidery thread for rosebuds
13 cm of 5 mm wide elastic

### Dress

1. Make patterns (*see Fig. 3*). Cut two yokes in plain cotton, two sleeves, one front and two backs in printed cotton.
2. Sew yokes together from back at (A) around neckline to other side. Trim and nick seam and corners. Turn to right side and press.
3. Using a gathering stitch, sew lace to front and back skirts across top. Gather sections to fit yokes. Press facings to wrong side on back skirt pieces and sew to top back yokes *only* from back yoke seam to side. Fold back the under yoke over back skirt piece and sew in the same way. Trim seam and turn to right side. Sew front skirt to top yoke *only* and trim seam. Turn under seam allowance on under yoke and handsew to machining across yoke seam.
4. Gather sleeves across head to fit armhole. Sew and neaten seams. Sew lace to sleeve at hem, neaten seam. Make a row of shirring across sleeve, close to lace. Tie ends securely. Sew and neaten underarm and side seams. Press seams, then sew lace to dress at hem. Neaten seam and press. Place ribbon across bottom of front and back yokes, stitch to yokes along each side. Make a small bow and stitch at centre. Work three buttonholes at back and

sew on buttons. Embroider rosebuds on yoke following directions given for booties, below.

### Bonnet

1. Make pattern (*see Fig. 3*). Cut two brims in printed cotton, one crown in plain cotton. Cut interfacing for brim if required.
2. Sew brim pieces together around outer edge. Turn to right side and press. Baste raw edges together. Topstitch brim 5 mm from outer edge on right side. Press under 5 mm and then 8 mm along neck edge of crown and machine across, close to edge, to make a casing. Insert elastic and sew across both ends securely. Gather crown around outer edge and pull up to fit inner edge of brim. Sew with right side of crown facing top side of brim. Trim and neaten seams. Cut remaining ribbon in half and sew to each side of bonnet at neck edge.

## VEST AND BOOTIES

One ball 3-ply yarn
1 pr 2.75 (No. 12) knitting needles
one double-pointed needle
2.50 (No. 12) crochet hook
1 m of 5 mm wide ribbon

two colours stranded embroidery thread for rosebuds
*Note:* More yarn may be necessary to complete both items.

### Booties

Cast on 46 sts and knit 4 rows.
*Next row:* K1, P2, (K1, P2) rep to last st, K1.
*Next row:* K3, P1, (K2, P1) rep to last 3 sts, K3. Work 5 rows in rib.
*Next row:* K1 (P2 tog, P1, K2, P1) rep 6 times, P2 tog, K1 (38 sts).
*Next row—Eyelet:* (K1, yfwd, K2 tog) rep to last st, K1.
*Next row:* Knit.
*Divide for instep:* K24, turn.
*Next row:* K10, turn. Knit 15 rows. Break off yarn. Pick up 10 sts along side of instep, K10 across end. Using a double-pointed needle, pick up 10 sts along other side of instep, K14 (58 sts). Knit 10 rows.
*Heel and toe shaping:* 1st row: K2 tog, K26 twice, K2 tog (55 sts).
*2nd row:* K5, K2 tog, pmon, K15, pmon, K2 tog, K7, K2 tog, pmon, K15, pmon, K2 tog, K5 (51 sts).
*3rd row:* Knit.
*4th row:* Knit to within 2 sts of first marker, K2 tog, knit to second marker, K2 tog, knit to within 2 sts of third

*Nightie*

marker, K2 tog, knit to fourth marker, K2 tog, knit to end of row (47 sts). Rep 3rd and 4th rows twice (39 sts).

*Next row:* Remove markers, K1, K2 tog, K14, K2 tog, K1, K2 tog, K14, K2 tog, K1.

*Next row:* Knit.

*Next row:* K2 tog, K13, K2 tog, K1, K2 tog, K13, K2 tog, K1. Cast off.

*To make up:* Using a small backstitch, sew up sole and back. Crochet shell edge around leg * 2 ch, 2 tr into first stitch, miss next st, sl st into next st. Rep from * around.

Embroider a tiny rosebud at front (*see p. 7*). **Work three bullion stitches in a triangle, then one larger in the centre.** Work lazy daisy stitches in contrast colour around rosebud. Thread ribbon through eyelets.

## Vest

Cast on 50 sts and work in rib of K2, P2, for 12 cm.

*Shoulder strap:* Work 8 cm on the first 12 sts. Break off yarn and slip sts on to holder. Join yarn where strap commenced. Cast off 26 sts in rib and work rem sts to correspond with other strap. Cast on 26 sts for back and work the 12 sts from holder (50 sts). Work back to correspond with front. Cast off in rib.

*To make up:* Sew up sides leaving an opening for armholes. Make neck edging by working 1 row dc, then work eyelet row, 1 tr, 1 ch, miss 1 st, rep around; then shell edge as for bootees. For armholes crochet shell edge only. Thread yarn cord at neck.

# ANGEL TOP AND LEGGINGS

*Note:* Leggings have been designed to fit over nappy and pilchers.

Two 25 g balls 5 ply apricot yarn for leggings
three 25 g balls 5 ply white yarn and small quantity left-over apricot yarn for angel top
1 pr 3 mm (No. 11) knitting needles
set of four double-pointed needles 2.75 mm (No. 12) for yoke
2.50 mm (No. 12) crochet hook
one 8 mm button
*Tension:* 6 sts and 9 rows to 2 cm.

## Leggings

*Right leg:* Using 3 mm needles cast on 42 sts in apricot.

*Vest, pilchers over nappy, and booties*

*1st row:* K1, (P1, K1 into back of st) rep to last st, K1.

*2nd row:* K1, (P1 into back of st, K1) rep to end of row. Rep these two rows once*.

*Note:* When turning, bring yarn to front of work, slip next st on to righthand needle, take yarn to back of work, slip the st back on to left-hand needle, then turn; this avoids holes.

*1st row:* Knit.
*2nd row:* K1, P to last st, K1.
*3rd row:* K10, turn.
*4th and alt rows:* P to last st, K1.
*5th row:* K16, turn.
*7th row:* K22, turn. St st 27 rows, end purl row * *.

Inc first and last st in next and foll 6th row (46 sts). St st 3 rows. Cast off 3 sts at beg of next 2 rows. Dec at each end of next and foll knit rows until 36 sts rem. St st 29 rows ending purl row. Dec at each end of next row. Purl 1 row * *

*Divide for instep: 1st row:* K28, K2 tog, turn.

*2nd row:* K1, P6, K1, turn. Work 8 rows on these 8 sts. Break off yarn. With right side of work facing, join in yarn and knit up 5 sts along side of instep, knit across 8 instep sts, knit up 5 sts along other side of instep, then knit across rem 4 sts (43 sts). Knit 11 rows.

*To shape foot: 1st row:* K8, K2 tog, K1, K2 tog, K13 (K2 tog, K1) 3 times, K8 (38 sts).
*2nd, 4th and 6th rows:* Knit.
*3rd row:* K7, K2 tog, K1, K2 tog, K12, K2 tog, K1, K2 tog, K9 (34 sts).
*5th row:* K6, K2 tog, K1, K2 tog, K10, K2 tog, K1, K2 tog, K8 (30 sts).
*7th row:* K5, K2 tog, K1, K2 tog, K8, K2 tog, K1, K2 tog, K7 (26 sts). Knit 1 row. Cast off.

*Left leg:* Work as for right leg to *.
*1st and alt rows:* Knit.
*2nd row:* K1, P10, turn.
*4th row:* K1, P16, turn.
*6th row:* K1, P22, turn. St st 28 rows, ending purl row.
Work as for right leg from * * to * *.

*Divide for instep: 1st row:* K12, K2 tog, turn.

*2nd row:* K1, P6, K1, turn. Work 8 rows on these 8 sts. Break off yarn. With right side of work facing, join in yarn and knit up 5 sts along side of instep, knit across 8 instep sts, knit up 5 sts along other side of instep, then knit across rem 20 sts (43 sts). Knit 11 rows.

*To shape foot: 1st row:* K9 (K2 tog, K1) 3 times, K12, K2 tog, K1, K2 tog, K8 (38 sts).
*2nd, 4th and 6th rows:* Knit.

*Angel top and leggings*

3rd row: K9, K2 tog, K1, K2 tog, K12, K2 tog, K1, K2 tog, K7 (34 sts).
5th row: K8, K2 tog, K1, K2 tog, K10, K2 tog, K1, K2 tog, K6 (30 sts).
7th row: K7, K2 tog, K1, K2 tog, K8, K2 tog, K1, K2 tog, K5 (26 sts). Knit 1 row. Cast off.

## Angel top

*Sleeves:* Using 3 mm needles cast on 28 sts in white. Knit 2 rows.
3rd row: K8 (inc 1, K1) 6 times, K8 (34 sts).
4th row: Purl.
5th row: Knit to last 5 sts, turn (see Note for leggings).
6th row: Purl to last 5 sts, turn.
7th row: Knit to end of row.
8th row: Purl. Rep last 4 rows 10 times. Inc first and last st in purl row foll 4th and 6th turns (38 sts). St st 4 rows without turning. Cast off 3 sts at beg of next 2 rows. Dec first and last st in next and foll knit rows (28 sts). St st 7 rows. Slip sts on to holder, break off yarn.

*Front:* Cast on 60 sts in white. Knit 3 rows.
Next row: Purl. Work in st st for 10 cm *.
Next row: Cast off 3 sts at beg of next 2 rows. Dec first and last st in next and foll knit rows to 50 sts. Purl 1 row.
*Right side shaping: 1st row:* K18, turn.

2nd, 4th and 6th rows: Purl to end of row.
3rd row: K12, turn.
5th row: K6, turn.
7th row: K6, K2 tog, (K4, K2 tog) twice, knit to end of row.
*Left side shaping: 1st row:* P18, turn.
2nd, 4th and 6th rows: Knit to end of row.
3rd row: P12, turn.
5th row: P6, turn.
7th row: P6, P2 tog, (P4, P2 tog) twice, purl to end of row * * (44 sts). Break off yarn. Place sts on holder.
*Back:* Work as for front to *. Cast off 3 sts at the beg of next row, K27, turn. Purl to end of row. Dec at beg of next 2 knit rows (25 sts). Purl 1 row. Follow directions given for right front side shaping above then purl 1 row. Break off yarn.

*To complete left side:* Join yarn at centre, knit to end of row. Cast off 3 sts at the beg of next row. Dec at end of next 2 knit rows (25 sts). Follow directions given for left front side shaping to * *, do not break off yarn.
*Yoke:* Change to double-pointed needles. With right side facing, beg at centre back.
*1st row:* K1 (K1 into back of st, P1) rep to last st. Knit last st of left side back together with first st of sleeve. Cont in rib across sleeve, K2 tog (into back of st) at centre. Join front to sleeve in same way. Cont in rib across front, K2 tog at centre front. Join in next sleeve in same way, K2 tog at centre of sleeve. Join in right side back in same way, rib to end of row (133 sts).
*2nd row:* K1 (P1 into back of st, K1) rep to end of row. Cont in rib without shaping for 4 cm.
*Next row:* K2 tog across row, K1. Cast off purlwise.

*To make up: Angel top:* Press lightly on wrong side. Sew armhole seams, then underarm and side seams. Work one row double crochet in white around back opening. Omit last 2 double crochet and work 3 chain for button loop.
*Crochet edging: Hem and sleeves:* With right side facing, work 1 tr, 1 ch into first st, sl st into next st, rep to end.
*Neck:* Work 1 row dc.
*Next row:* 1 tr, 1 ch into second st, sl st into next st, rep to end.
*Leggings:* Sew up front, back, leg and foot seams. Insert hat elastic at waist if necessary.

# CARRY-BASKET SET
*(Length 50 cm, width 25 cm, depth 14 cm)*

The basket is made in heavy quality gabardine and has a masonite base. The sides are stiffened with vilene and rows of parallel machine stitching. The mattress and pillow are made in plain cotton and filled with polyester wadding. The liner is made in printed cotton, trimmed with broderie anglaise.

## Basket

70 × 150 cm wide gabardine
136 × 30 cm wide piece iron-on vilene
25 × 50 cm wide piece of 3 mm masonite or heavy cardboard
sandpaper
sewing thread to match for topstitching

## Liner

40 × 90 cm wide printed cotton
3 m broderie anglaise
1 m of 5 mm ribbon
shirring elastic

## Pillow, mattress and quilt

50 × 90 cm wide plain cotton
30 × 90 cm wide printed cotton
50 × 90 cm wide piece polyester wadding
1 m broderie anglaise

## Basket

1. For base, make a paper pattern of curve (see Fig. 3) and mark on to the corners of masonite. Cut curves and smooth edges with sandpaper. Make a paper pattern of base, adding a 1 cm seam allowance. Using this pattern cut two from gabardine.
2. For sides, cut one 136 × 30 cm wide piece each in gabardine and iron-on vilene. Cut one 136 × 4.5 cm wide piece for reinforcing top and two 30 × 10 cm wide pieces for handle from gabardine.
3. Press iron-on vilene to wrong side of side piece. Press in half lengthwise with right side outside.
4. Press handle strips in half with wrong side inside, the press raw eges in to meet at centre. Machine stitch near edges on both sides, then sew two more rows evenly along centre of handle.
5. Open side piece and mark into quarters with chalk on centre fold, which becomes top edge. Exclude 1 cm seam allowance at each end when measuring. Position handles with raw ends 1 cm below fold, and 6 cm either side of chalk marks nearest ends (see Fig. 4).

6. Prepare reinforcing band by pressing 1 cm to wrong side along one side. With right sides facing, place raw edge of band 1 cm below foldline of side piece. Machine along foldline and press band down on to right side to cover ends of handle. Baste folded edge of band to side piece (*see Fig. 5*).

7. Baste ends together with right sides inside to make a circle and check that it fits the base, then stitch. Press seam open and fold in half with handles at top. Press and baste raw edges together at the bottom. Begin decorative stitching along band at top to match stitching on handles. Keeping rows the same distance apart, continue to bottom (*see Figs 6A, 6B*).

8. Turn inside out and sew to outer base with 1 cm seam allowance. Fold sides of basket towards centre and place inner and outer base together with right sides facing. Sew on same stitching line. Leave one end open from beginning of curve on each side. Trim seams and turn to right side. Slip masonite into base and handstitch around opening. Turn basket right side out (*see Fig. 6B*).

## Basket liner

1. Cut two 20 × 90 cm wide pieces from printed cotton; four 27 cm and one 180 cm lengths of lace; four 25 cm lengths of ribbon.

2. To make handle openings, mark a line in chalk on right side of one piece printed cotton, 27 cm long and 5.5 cm from one edge. Pin two pieces of lace with raw edges meeting along this line (*see Fig. 7*). Sew lace 5 mm from edge, stopping 1 cm from ends. Cut fabric between stitching and zigzag raw edges. Press seam to wrong side. Sew a row of shirring along seam allowance on both sides. Tie off ends securely. Sew ends of lace together with seam on the inside of opening. Handsew raw edges between lace at ends to reinforce. Make opening for other side in same way.

3. Sew the two sides together at one end. Sew lace along outer edge. Zigzag seam and press to wrong side. Sew a row of shirring along seam allowance. Press 5 mm to wrong side along bottom edge of liner and sew a row of shirring with elastic on the wrong side. Sew ends of liner together, securing shirring threads firmly. Sew ribbons to both sides of handle openings.

## Mattress

1. Using pattern for masonite base, omit 1 cm seam allowance and cut two

pieces from plain cotton. Cut one piece polyester wadding, 1 cm smaller than the fabric.

2. Sew with right sides together, leaving an opening on one side. Trim seams, turn to right side and press. Insert wadding and handsew across the opening.

## Pillow

1. Cut two 14 × 21 cm pieces plain cotton. Cut around corners to form a curve. Cut two pieces polyester wadding, 1 cm smaller than fabric.

2. Gather lace to fit around edge, allowing extra fullness at corners. Sew lace to one side of pillow, with right sides and raw edges together. Sew to other side with lace inside. Leave opening for wadding. Trim seams and turn to right side. Insert wadding, handsew across opening.

## Quilt

1. Cut two 30 × 35 cm wide pieces printed cotton and curve corners. Cut one piece polyester wadding, 1 cm smaller than the fabric.

2. Make as for mattress, then quilt by machine through all layers, 3 cm from edges.

*Carrybasket set*

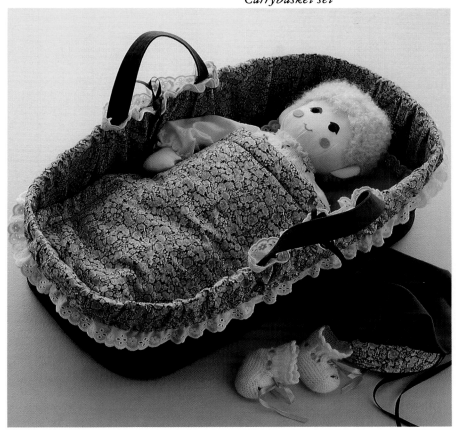

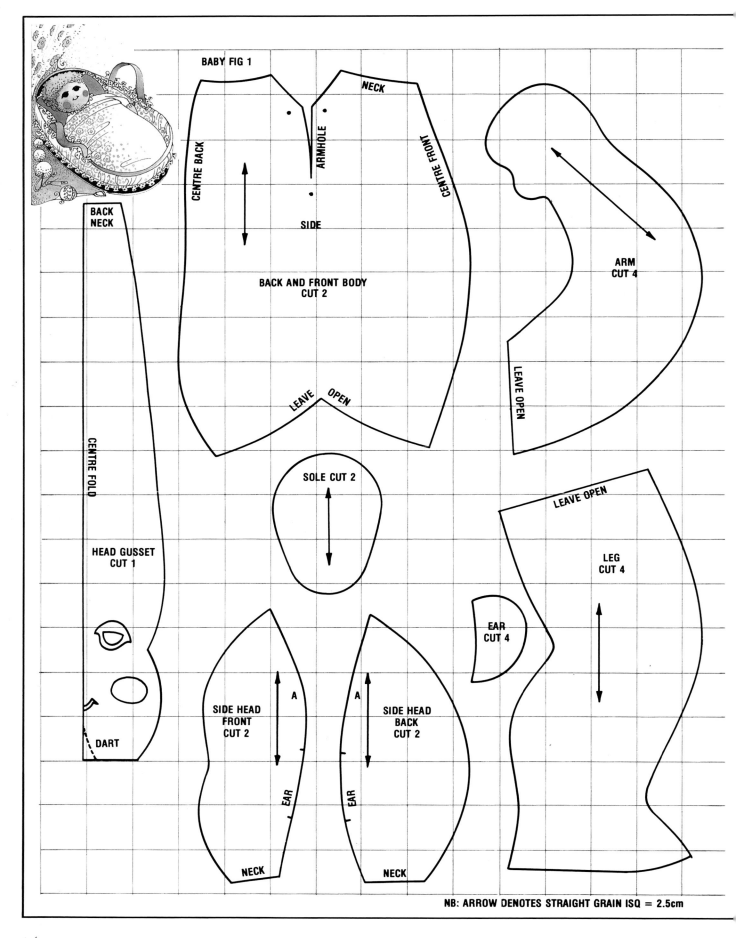

BABY FIG 1

NECK

CENTRE BACK

ARMHOLE

CENTRE FRONT

SIDE

ARM
CUT 4

BACK AND FRONT BODY
CUT 2

LEAVE OPEN

LEAVE OPEN

BACK
NECK

CENTRE FOLD

SOLE CUT 2

LEAVE OPEN

HEAD GUSSET
CUT 1

LEG
CUT 4

EAR
CUT 4

DART

SIDE HEAD
FRONT
CUT 2

A

A

SIDE HEAD
BACK
CUT 2

EAR

EAR

NECK

NECK

NB: ARROW DENOTES STRAIGHT GRAIN ISQ = 2.5cm

14

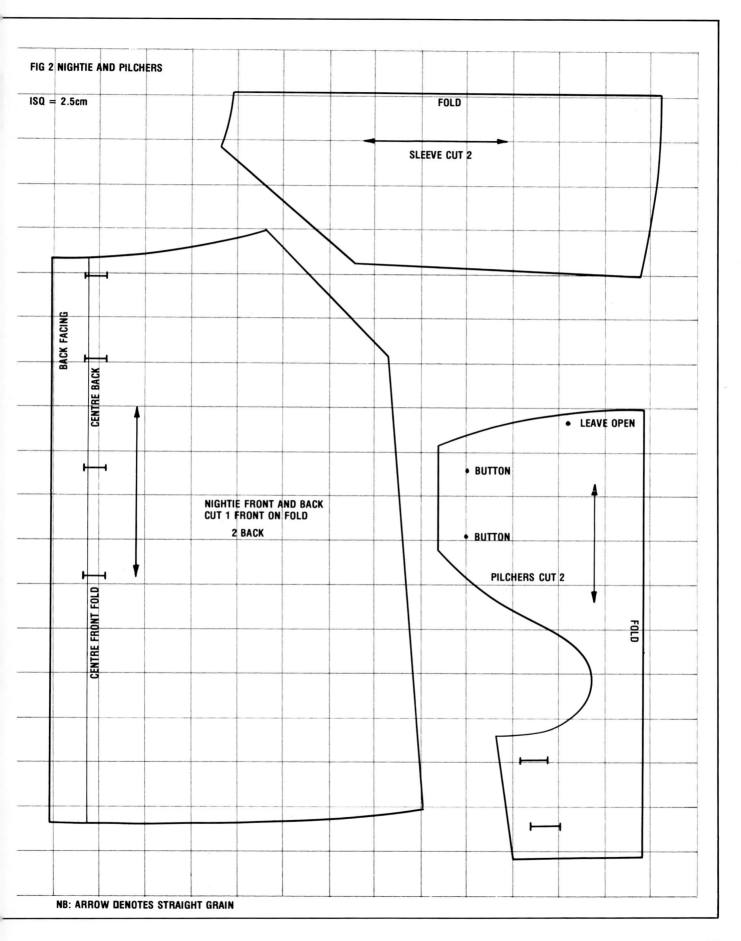

FIG 2 NIGHTIE AND PILCHERS

ISQ = 2.5cm

FOLD

SLEEVE CUT 2

BACK FACING

CENTRE BACK

NIGHTIE FRONT AND BACK
CUT 1 FRONT ON FOLD
2 BACK

CENTRE FRONT FOLD

LEAVE OPEN

• BUTTON

• BUTTON

PILCHERS CUT 2

FOLD

NB: ARROW DENOTES STRAIGHT GRAIN

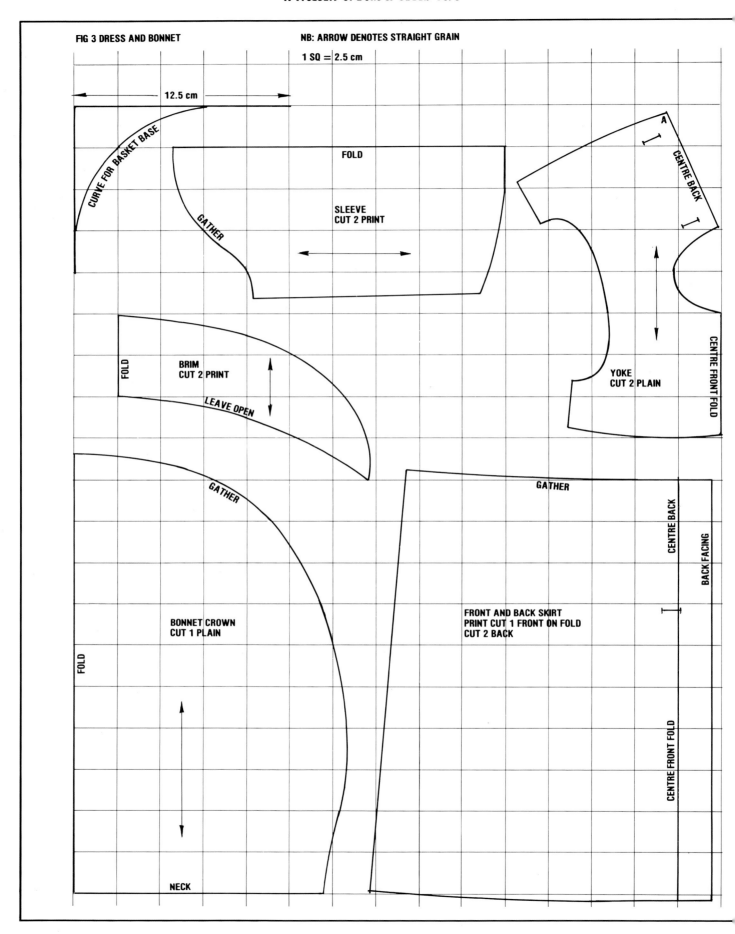

FIG 3 DRESS AND BONNET

NB: ARROW DENOTES STRAIGHT GRAIN

1 SQ = 2.5 cm

12.5 cm

CURVE FOR BASKET BASE

FOLD

SLEEVE
CUT 2 PRINT

GATHER

A

CENTRE BACK

BRIM
CUT 2 PRINT

FOLD

LEAVE OPEN

YOKE
CUT 2 PLAIN

CENTRE FRONT FOLD

GATHER

GATHER

BONNET CROWN
CUT 1 PLAIN

FOLD

CENTRE BACK

BACK FACING

FRONT AND BACK SKIRT
PRINT CUT 1 FRONT ON FOLD
CUT 2 BACK

CENTRE FRONT FOLD

NECK

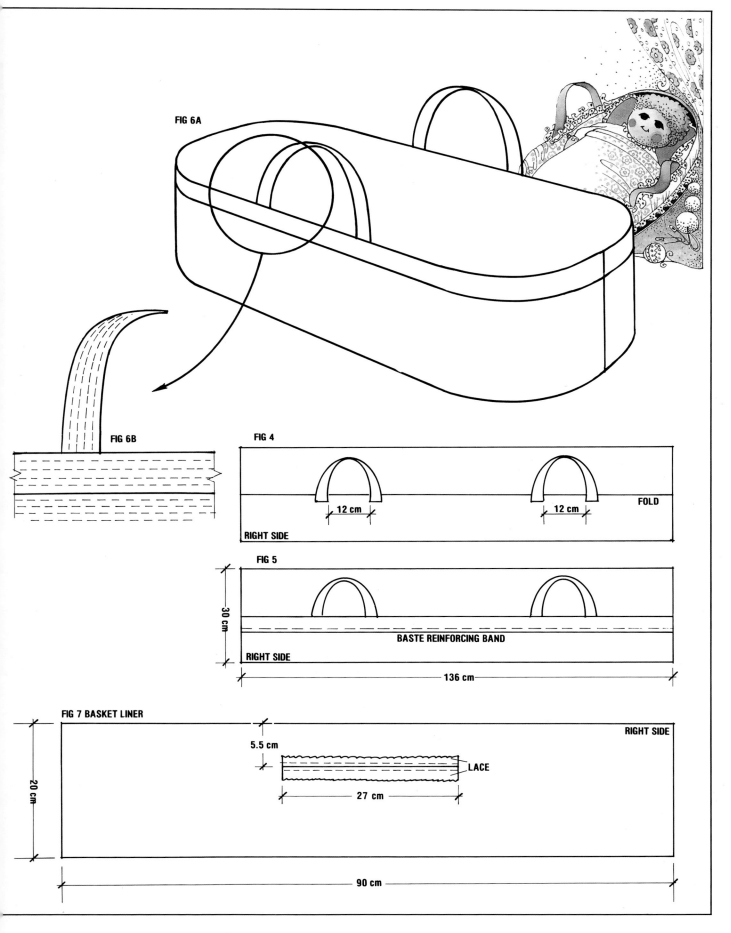

FIG 6A

FIG 6B

FIG 4

12 cm          12 cm          **FOLD**

**RIGHT SIDE**

FIG 5

30 cm

**BASTE REINFORCING BAND**

**RIGHT SIDE**

136 cm

**FIG 7 BASKET LINER**

**RIGHT SIDE**

5.5 cm

LACE

27 cm

20 cm

90 cm

# A Doll Family in Colonial Costume

DESIGNED BY ELIZABETH RUSSELL

These attractive little people are dressed in clothes such as those worn by middle-class settlers during the first half of the 19th century.

To enlarge patterns, rule up a sheet of brown paper in squares to the scale indicated. Carefully mark on pattern, drawing from square to square. When you are satisfied with the shape cut out the enlarged pattern. All garments have 6 mm seam allowances with the exception of some pieces cut in felt where no allowance has been necessary. This has been indicated on pattern pieces, so if you wish to use fabric other than felt, remember to make the necessary adjustments. All shoes have been made in felt and it is only necessary to take a very narrow seam as indicated. When sewing felt, trim seams very fine to remove excess bulk. Leave hair and features till the clothes have been made up. The character of the doll will be more developed and colouring and expression easier to decide.

## THE DOLL

Mark out body pieces on prepared paper. It is important to note that *no* seam allowance has been included on the body pieces. The pattern pieces are placed on the fabric and very lightly marked around with a sharp pencil. The fine pencil line is used as a sewing guide. This method gives a well-shaped doll, but be careful with the pencil, as a heavy line will show through on the light-coloured fabric. When cutting out allow 6 mm seam allowance all round.

### To make up

After cutting the required number of pieces, pin or tack them together. Use a small machine stitch and sew around on the marked line. Remember to leave head and body open at neck; legs and arms at the top. Nick all curved lines and trim away seams where necessary (between finger and thumb, around curves of head and shoulders). Turn

*Doll Family in Colonial Costume*

through and make sure the shapes are well pushed out to the seams.

### Stuffing

Stuff carefully and very firmly using only small pieces of filling. The more care you take, the better the shape will be. Use a knitting needle or a piece of dowelling, sharpened to a blunt point at one end to move filling into small difficult areas. The stuffing settles down after some time so it needs to be very firm. A length of cane is inserted into neck and body to strengthen neck and prevent it getting wobbly later on.

### Head

Partly stuff head and insert cane to a depth of half its length. Stuff firmly around cane and down neck.

### Body

Stuff body to about the shoulders. Poke a hole in the stuffing with your finger and insert the end of cane protruding from head. This is a little tricky and you may need to remove the cane and stuff the body more firmly, then try again until you are satisfied you can complete the rest of the stuffing without too much difficulty. The head and body are eased together until stitching lines meet as indicated on pattern. Pin all around. Sew neatly and firmly across front from seam to seam with a double thread. Remove pins across back and add more stuffing until very firm. Pin back up again and sew across. Sew around neck again for extra firmness and neatness.

### Legs and Arms

Stuff legs and arms firmly, taking care with the hands. Stuff the last 12 mm lightly, turn in seam allowance and sew across. Sew legs and arms firmly with double thread in positions as indicated. The legs can be stuffed and machined into body first for extra strength if you wish. Pin them in across the bottom. Machine across several times on the outside and then stuff the body.

## GIRL

Flesh-coloured firm cotton 30 × 90 cm
polyester fibre filling
1 length cane 15 cm
white lawn 40 × 90 cm
printed cotton 40 × 90 cm
approximately one 25 g ball 4-ply bright yellow wool
scraps iron-on vilene
1 m narrow ribbon
1 small button
3 press-studs
length of lace 12 mm × 50 cm
scraps black and blue felt
red and black embroidery threads
scraps of cotton interlock (you can use a child's sock or an old fine singlet)
sewing cottons to match
length of elastic
4 m ric-rac braid

### Dress

Cut from printed fabric: two sleeves, one front bodice, two back bodices, one neckband. Cut one piece 56 × 19 cm for skirt.

### Petticoat

Cut one piece white lawn 50 × 13 cm.

### To make up

Join back and front bodices along shoulder seams. Machine a narrow hem across bottom of sleeves. Put a gathering thread around top of each sleeve and two rows across sleeve 6 mm above hem edge. Pull up gathering thread of sleeves to fit bodice armhole and machine them in. Pull up gathering threads across sleeve to approx. 11 cm. Machine across to hold gathering in place. Fit bodice on doll. Be sure sleeve can be pulled over the hand. Remove and sew down side and underarm seams; neaten raw edges of back facings. With right sides together sew one side of neck band around neck edge. Fold band in half and sew across each end. Turn under a small hem and slip-stitch down.

### Skirt

Machine up centre back of petticoat, leaving an opening of approximately 7 cm. Using a narrow zigzag stitch, sew on lace edging around lower edge. Put a gathering stitch around waist edge. Machine up centre back of printed skirt leaving an opening of 7 cm. Neaten lower edge and put a gathering stitch around waist. Slip-stitch petticoat to skirt around back opening. Gather petticoat and skirt to fit bodice and then sew them together. Sew skirt to bodice. Turn back bodice facing and sew across at waist. Sew press-studs down centre back. Sew up hem 2 cm deep. Press.

## Bonnet

From printed cotton: cut two brim, one crown, one circle. From iron-on vilene: cut brim, one crown, one circle. Iron the vilene on to one piece of brim, crown and circle. Sew ric-rac braid around outer and inner edges of brim. Join up brim and crown at centre back. Sew crown to brim around lower edge. Fit circle to hat, tack around carefully and machine. Join brim facing at centre back. With right sides together, tack and sew around outer edge. Turn facing to under-side. Trim all seams and zigzag facing to upper brim along seam edge. Press. Decorate each side with loops of ribbon leaving long ends to be tied under the chin.

## Apron

Using white lawn cut two bodice pieces; one piece 13 × 21 cm for skirt. Cut two pieces 41 × 3 cm for ties.

For frilling, cut a strip of lawn approximately 3 × 81 cm. Edge one side with ric-rac braid and put two rows of gathering down the other side. Frilling should be 2 cm wide when finished (this includes the ric-rac). You can use broderie or lace edging also if you wish. Sew frilling along each side of outer edge of front piece and across the bottom of apron skirt. Sew a small hem 3 mm wide down each side of apron skirt and put a gathering stitch across the top. Gather to 12 cm. The skirt will extend 2 cm each side of bodice.

## Ties

Turn under a 3 mm wide hem down one side, across bottom and along remaining side to 5 cm from the end. Sew the tie ends to each side of front piece as indicated, with the raw edge to the bottom. Sew front and ties along gathered edge of skirt. With right sides together, place the two front pieces together and sew around neck edge. Trim seam and turn through to the right side. Turn under raw edges around outer edge and slip-stitch down. Make a buttonhole at centre back and sew on a small button. Press.

## Drawers

Cut out a pair of drawers in white lawn. Sew down side seams. Make a length of frilling as for apron or use broderie or lace. Sew two rows of frilling to each leg. Machine inside leg seam. Make a

12 mm hem at waist and thread elastic through. Press.

## Stockings

Cut two pieces from interlock cotton required length. Zigzag a narrow hem along top edge. Pin around each leg and foot. Remove from leg and zigzag down the seam. Cut away excess material.

## Shoes

Cut four pieces in black felt. Sew around each pair with a narrow seam. Turn through to right side. It is a good idea to sew the shoes onto the leg.

## Hair and features

Use one ball or more of bright yellow wool, depending on length of hair you desire. Our doll has her hair cut in 45 cm lengths. Cut wool into required lengths and make a wig. Sew firmly to head. Catch hair to side of face first, then catch an underneath layer all around head so that the pink head doesn't show through hair. Leave a top layer to hang loose. Trim across bottom.

**Hair:** It is usually best to make a small wig first; unless you have chosen a particular style i.e.—Boy. The hair is sewn to a short length of tape and the tape is sewn to the head to give a firm finish.

**To make a wig:** Cut lengths of wool required measurement. Measure the width you will need across the centre of the head or at parting. Begin at about 2.5 cm down on the forehead. This should give a good shape to the face. Cut a length of bias binding or tape the colour of body or hair, whichever you are able to match best. Lay hair on tape and machine across several times (see **diagram on page 23**). Turn under ends of tape and pin to head. Sew tape very firmly to head down each side. Arrange hair in the style you have chosen and catch hair to head with matching cotton where necessary.

**Features:** Mark position of eyes on face after hair has been arranged. This will be a guide in deciding the other features. Cut two small circles of felt in black, blue or brown 1 cm in diameter. Pin them to the face first. They can then be moved around until you are satisfied the position is right. Sew them on with matching cotton, concealing the stitches. Add small eyelashes with a single thread of black embroidery cotton to the face of woman and girl. Omit them from the man and boy. Next, with a sharp pencil, lightly draw on a mouth

and eyebrows. These are worked with a single thread of embroidery cotton in stem stitch. Black thread for eyebrows, red for mouth. Add two small knots of black cotton above mouth for nose.

# WOMAN

Flesh-coloured firm cotton 40 × 90 cm
polyester fibre filling
1 length cane 15 cm
printed cotton 40 × 90 cm
white lawn 30 × 90 cm
scrap of voile or organdie
4 m lace
approximately one 25 g ball 4-ply brown wool
3 small black buttons or beads
scraps of black felt
black and red embroidery thread
sewing cottons to match
ribbon 12 mm wide and scraps 6 mm wide
length of elastic

## Dress

Cut from printed fabric: one front bodice, two back bodices, two sleeves. Cut 1 piece 29 × 71 cm for the skirt. Cut 1 bodice yoke from voile.

## Petticoat

Cut 1 piece white lawn 23 × 54 cm.

## To make up

Tack voile yoke over front bodice. Machine down with a fine zigzag stitch, adding a gathered lace edging at the same time. Join back and front bodices along shoulder seams. Neaten back facings and press under. Sew gathered lace across bottom of each sleeve. Put a gathering thread around top. Gather to fit bodice armhole and machine into bodice. Fit bodice on doll. Be sure sleeve can be pulled over the hand. Remove and sew down side and under-arm seams. Sew edge of gathered lace around neck with a fine zigzag stitch.

## Skirt

Follow instructions given for **Girl** and make up skirt and petticoat. Join to the bodice. Fit dress on doll to get length you desire. Add two rows of lace. The first 4 cm from raw edge, the second 9 cm from raw edge. Neaten hem and sew up 12 cm deep. Add three small buttons or beads to front yoke and three press-studs down the centre back. Press. Add sash of ribbon around waist.

## Drawers

Cut out a pair of drawers in white lawn. Sew down side seams. Add three rows of lace as marked on pattern. Machine inside leg seam. Make a 12 mm hem at waist and thread elastic through. Press.

## Cap

Cut out a circle of voile 13 cm in diameter. Machine-gather lace around edge with a fine zigzag stitch. Put a row of gathering 1 cm in from edge. Gather to required size. Sew around a second row of gathered lace over the gathering stitch. Make a small bow from narrow ribbon and sew to front. It is a good idea to sew cap to the hair when doll is finished. Make a bonnet for woman if you prefer but enlarge the pattern for **Girl** a little first.

## Shoes

Cut out four pieces in black felt. Sew around each pair with a narrow seam. Turn through to right side. Decorate with a bow, beads, or a small rosette of ribbon. Sew shoes to leg at the back.

## Hair and features

Following directions for **Girl**, cut a ball of dark brown wool into lengths of 56 cm. Cut an 11 cm piece of tape. Make a wig and sew to head. Tie hair with wool in two bunches at each side of head and sew firmly to head. Tie hair again 16 cm below that and trim off ends. Twist hair around like a rope and coil towards the face in a bun. Tuck in ends and sew firmly to head.

## BOY

Flesh-coloured firm cotton 30 × 90 cm
polyester fibre filling
1 length cane 15 cm
scraps gold corduroy
1 square of black felt 30 × 30 cm
scraps of interlock cotton
length of pleated sheer frilling 2 cm
  wide
one 25 g ball 4-ply light brown wool
18 small black beads
elastic
sewing threads to match

Cut out doll and make it up.

## Trousers

Cut one pair of trousers in gold corduroy. Sew together side seams and inside seams of each leg. Join legs together at centre seam. Make a 12 mm hem at waist. Thread through elastic. Fit trousers on the doll and mark length of leg. Remove and sew up the hem.

## Jacket

*Note:* When sewing felt trim seams very fine to remove excess bulk. Cut two front bodices, one back bodice, two sleeves from black felt.

*Girl in full costume*

## To make up

Decorate jacket by sewing two rows of stitches in black down centre back and either side of centre back as marked on the pattern. Sew two rows on each jacket front as marked. Join back and front bodice at shoulder seams. Trim seams. Put a gathering thread around top of sleeves. Ease into armhole and sew around. Fit jacket on doll. Make sure sleeve can be pulled over the hand. Remove and sew down side and under-arm seams. Trim seams. Sew on six beads down centre front and cut small matching buttonholes. Sew six beads down each row of stitching on fronts as marked on pattern.

## Neck ruff

Gather neck frilling to fit neck. If already gathered fit around neck and cut to required length. Sew a small hook on one end and embroider a loop on the other.

## Stockings

Cut two pieces from interlock cotton required length. Zigzag a narrow hem along top edge. Pin around each leg and foot. Remove from the leg and zigzag down seam. Cut away excess material.

## Shoes

Cut four pieces in black felt. Sew around each pair with a narrow seam. Turn through to the right side. It is a good idea to sew the shoes onto the leg.

## Hair and features

Following directions for **Girl** and using light brown wool, cut a long length of wool approximately 3 metres. Fold into four thicknesses. Sew to head in small loops with a double thread of matching cottons. Start at centre of forehead, about 2 cm down on forehead. Work in a line down the side of face, across back and around to centre of forehead. This will set the hairline and the shape of the face, so be careful to look often at the shape you are forming. Continue working around the head until it has been covered completely.

# MAN

Flesh-coloured firm cotton 40 × 90 cm
polyester fibre filling
1 length cane 15 cm
large scraps black/white check wool
large scrap white lawn
1 square royal blue felt 40 × 50 cm
scrap of beige felt
approximately half a ball 4-ply black wool
7 small black buttons or beads
narrow black ribbon
elastic
sewing threads to match

Cut out the doll and make it up.

## Trousers

Cut one pair of trousers in check wool. Sew together side seams and inside seams of each leg. Join legs together at centre seam. Make a 12 mm hem at waist. Thread through elastic. Fit trousers on doll and mark length of leg. Remove and sew up hems. Make two narrow straps 6 mm wide from check wool. These straps will be fitted over the foot and sewn to either side of trouser leg.
*Note:* When sewing felt, trim seams very fine to remove excess bulk.

## Waistcoat

Cut two fronts, one back from beige felt. Sew together at shoulders and fit on doll. Sew down side seams. Trim seams. Finish with four small black buttons or beads. Cut four small button-holes with a sharp pair of scissors.

## Coat

Cut two front bodices, one back bodice, two sleeves, two skirt pieces, one back underpleat from royal blue felt, one collar from black felt.

## To make up

Decorate back bodice by sewing two rows of fine stitching in black cotton down centre back. Sew two more rows either side of centre back as marked on the pattern. Join back and front bodice at shoulder seams. Trim seams. Put a gathering thread around the top of sleeves. Ease into armhole and sew around. Trim seams. Hand-sew collar to neck edge. Fit the bodice on doll over the waistcoat and trousers. Make sure sleeve can be pulled over the hand. Remove and sew down side and under-arm seams. Trim seams. Join the three pieces of coat skirt together and press in pleat at centre back. Stitch pleat at waist to hold in place. Put a row of gathering either side of centre back as marked on pattern. Gather up skirt to fit bodice and join together. Trim seams and press. Sew on three small buttons or beads. Cut three small buttonholes with a sharp pair of scissors.

## Cravat

Cut cravat from white lawn. Neaten edge with a narrow hem. Cravat is tied as a scarf around the neck. It is held in place with a narrow ribbon which is tied around over cravat and finished in a small bow at the front.

## Boots

Cut out four pieces in black felt. Sew around each pair with a narrow seam. Turn through to right side.

## Hair and features

Following directions for **Girl** cut required amount of black wool into lengths of 25 cm. Make a wig and sew to the head. If you want a smooth head of hair, catch it down lightly all around about halfway down the head. Try to conceal stitches. Trim hair to desired length and catch carefully 6 mm from the bottom. To make beard, sew small loops of wool around the sides of face and chin. Make thick side-burns and shape it down to two rows across the chin.

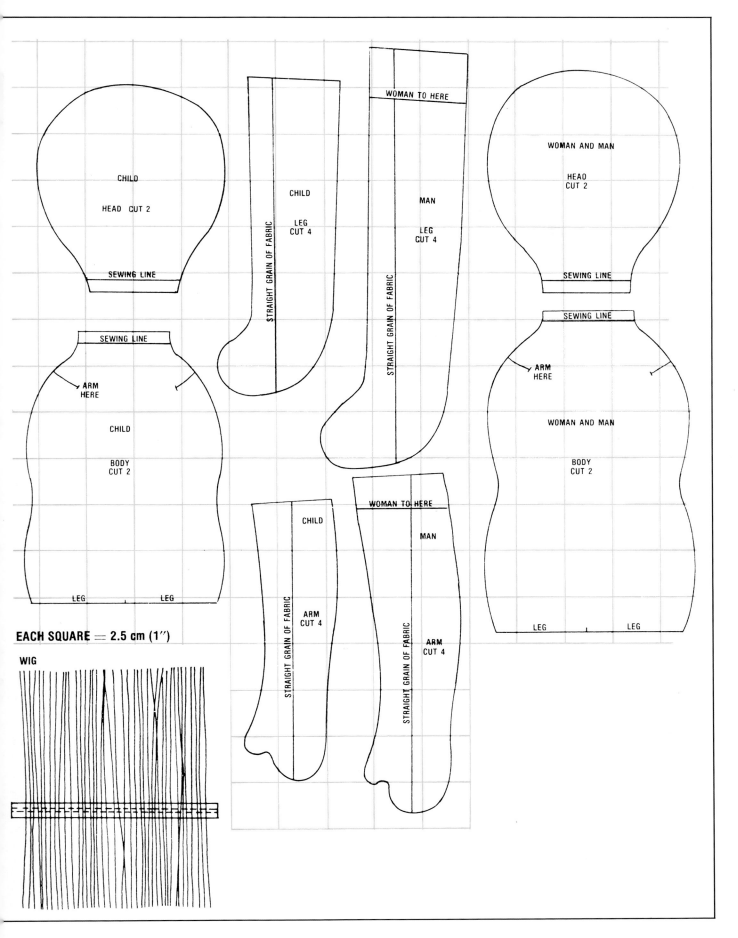

CHILD

HEAD  CUT 2

SEWING LINE

CHILD

LEG
CUT 4

STRAIGHT GRAIN OF FABRIC

WOMAN TO HERE

MAN

LEG
CUT 4

STRAIGHT GRAIN OF FABRIC

WOMAN AND MAN

HEAD
CUT 2

SEWING LINE

SEWING LINE

SEWING LINE

ARM
HERE

ARM
HERE

CHILD

BODY
CUT 2

WOMAN AND MAN

BODY
CUT 2

LEG          LEG

LEG          LEG

**EACH SQUARE = 2.5 cm (1″)**

WIG

CHILD

STRAIGHT GRAIN OF FABRIC

ARM
CUT 4

WOMAN TO HERE

MAN

STRAIGHT GRAIN OF FABRIC

ARM
CUT 4

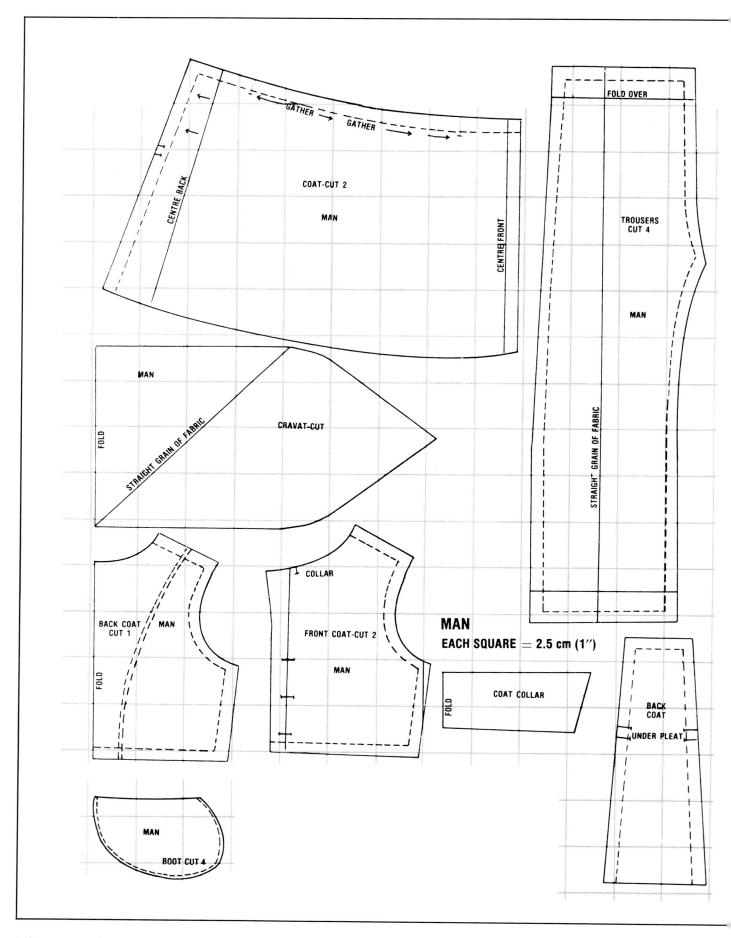

CENTRE BACK

COAT-CUT 2

MAN

CENTRE FRONT

GATHER → GATHER →

FOLD OVER

TROUSERS CUT 4

MAN

STRAIGHT GRAIN OF FABRIC

MAN

FOLD

STRAIGHT GRAIN OF FABRIC

CRAVAT-CUT

COLLAR

BACK COAT CUT 1    MAN

FOLD

FRONT COAT-CUT 2

MAN

**MAN**

**EACH SQUARE = 2.5 cm (1″)**

FOLD    COAT COLLAR

BACK COAT

UNDER PLEAT

MAN

BOOT CUT 4

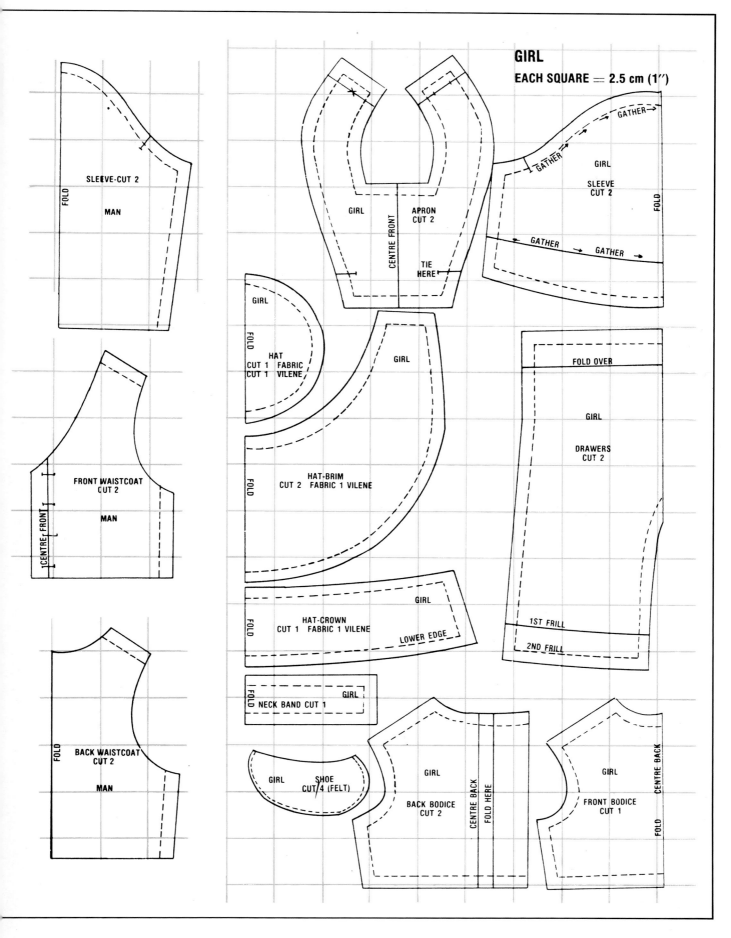

GIRL
EACH SQUARE = 2.5 cm (1")

SLEEVE-CUT 2
FOLD
MAN

FRONT WAISTCOAT
CUT 2
MAN
CENTRE FRONT

BACK WAISTCOAT
CUT 2
FOLD
MAN

GIRL
CENTRE FRONT
APRON
CUT 2
TIE HERE

GIRL
FOLD
HAT
CUT 1 FABRIC
CUT 1 VILENE

GIRL
HAT-BRIM
CUT 2 FABRIC 1 VILENE
FOLD

GIRL
HAT-CROWN
CUT 1 FABRIC 1 VILENE
FOLD
LOWER EDGE

GIRL
FOLD NECK BAND CUT 1

GIRL SHOE
CUT 4 (FELT)

GIRL
SLEEVE
CUT 2
FOLD
GATHER
GATHER
GATHER

FOLD OVER
GIRL
DRAWERS
CUT 2
1ST FRILL
2ND FRILL

GIRL
BACK BODICE
CUT 2
CENTRE BACK
FOLD HERE

GIRL
FRONT BODICE
CUT 1
CENTRE BACK
FOLD

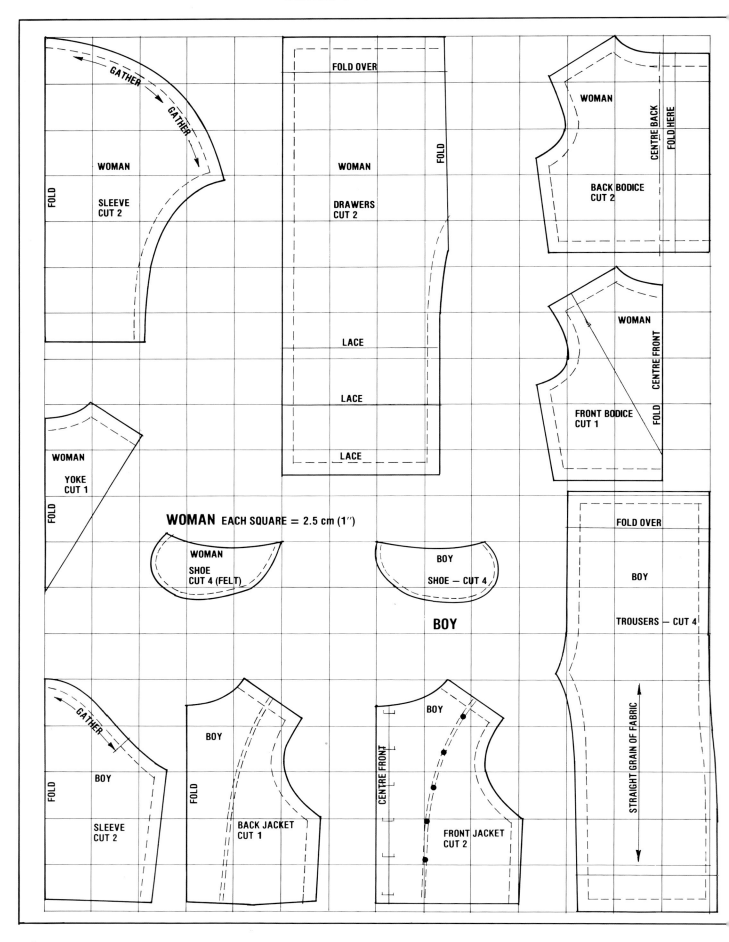

GATHER
GATHER

WOMAN
SLEEVE
CUT 2

FOLD

FOLD OVER

WOMAN
DRAWERS
CUT 2

FOLD

LACE

LACE

LACE

WOMAN
CENTRE BACK
FOLD HERE
BACK BODICE
CUT 2

WOMAN
CENTRE FRONT
FOLD
FRONT BODICE
CUT 1

WOMAN
YOKE
CUT 1

FOLD

**WOMAN** EACH SQUARE = 2.5 cm (1″)

WOMAN
SHOE
CUT 4 (FELT)

BOY
SHOE — CUT 4

**BOY**

FOLD OVER

BOY
TROUSERS — CUT 4

STRAIGHT GRAIN OF FABRIC

GATHER

BOY
SLEEVE
CUT 2

FOLD

BOY
BACK JACKET
CUT 1

FOLD

BOY
CENTRE FRONT
FRONT JACKET
CUT 2

*Three Sleepy Mice*

# Three Sleepy Mice

DESIGNED BY GWEN MERRILL

Knit these tiny toys, which can be slipped in and out of their sleeping bags.

Body and head (height 12 cm) are knitted in one piece with seam at centre back. Arms and ears are worked separately. Sleeping bag is knitted from the bottom in a simple check pattern. The pillow is knitted after centre back seam has been sewn.

*Abbreviations:* K — *Knit*; P — *Purl*; st(s) — *stitch(es)*; cont — *continue*; tog — *together*; st st — *stocking stitch*; inc — *increase*; dec — *decrease*; sl st — *slip stitch*; dc — *double crochet*; ch — *chain*; alt — *alternate*.

## MOUSE

Small quantities Patons Bluebell 5-ply yarn in bright colours
1 pr 2.75 mm (No. 12) knitting needles
tapestry needle
2.50 mm (No. 12) crochet hook
polyester fibre for filling
Cast on 16 sts for foot. Knit 6 rows. Break off yarn and rep for other foot. Change to body colour and knit across both feet. Knit 27 rows. Change to head colour, K16, inc 1 by knitting loop bet sts, K16 (33 sts).
*Next and alt rows:* Purl. *Next row:* K16, K3 times in next st, K16, (35 sts). Inc in this manner in central st in foll knit rows until 39 sts. *Next row:* P17, P2 tog, P1, P2 tog, P17 (37 sts). *Next row:* K15, K2 tog, K3, K2 tog, K15 (35 sts). *Next row:* P13, P2 tog, P5, P2 tog, P13 (33 sts). *Next row:* K11, K2 tog, K7, K2 tog, K11 (31 sts). *Next row:* P9, P2 tog, P9, P2 tog, P9 (29 sts).

### Cap

Change colour and knit 6 rows.
*Next row:* Change colour, K1, K2 tog, K5, K2 tog, K4, K2 tog, K3, K2 tog, K5, K2 tog, K1 (24 sts). *Next and alt rows:* Knit. *Next row:* K3, K2 tog, K3, K2 tog, K4, K2 tog, K3, K2 tog, K3 (20 sts). *Next row:* K3, (K2 tog, K2) 3 times, K2 tog, K3 (16 sts). *Next row:* K1, (K2 tog, K2) 3 times, K2 tog, K1 (12 sts). *Next row:* K2, (K2 tog) 4 times, K2 (8 sts). Knit 3 rows. *Next row:* (K2 tog) 4 times (4 sts). Knit 3 rows. *Next row:* K2 tog twice. *Next row:* K2 tog. Fasten off.

### Arm (work 2)

Cast on 12 sts. Knit 8 rows. Change colour knit 4 rows.
*Next row:* (K2 tog) 6 times. Cast off.

### Ear (crochet 2)

Ch 2. Work 5 dc in 2nd ch from hook, 1 ch, turn.
*Next row:* 2 dc in each dc (10 dc), 1 ch, turn.
*Next row:* 3 dc, work 2 dc in next dc, 2 dc, work 2 dc in next dc, 3 dc (12 dc), turn.
*Next row:* Sl st in next 2 dc, 2 dc, work 2 dc in next dc, 2 dc, work 2 dc in next dc, 2 dc, sl st in next 2 dc (14 dc), fasten off.

### To make up

Using tapestry needle and matching thread sew sides of feet and gather up cast-on edges. Sew back seam to neck. Weave a matching thread across first row of face on wrong side, leave ends on right side. Sew back head to beg of cap. Fill feet and body with small pieces of fibre, defining fat tummies and pointed nose. Do not fill cap. Pull in neck and secure threads. Sew back seam of cap. Sew arm seam, fill softly and sew to body at sides. Gather straight edge of ears and sew to sides of head below cap. Embroider nose, mouth and eyes in black following photograph. Make a pompon the size of a machine bobbin. Sew to end of cap.

## SLEEPING BAG

Cast on 27 sts in navy. Purl one row.
*2nd row:* Knit, inc in each st (54 sts). St st 3 rows.
*6th row:* K1 red, * sl 1 navy, K2 red * rep 16 times, sl 1 navy, K1 red.
*7th row:* P1 red, * sl 1 navy, P2 red * rep 16 times, sl 1 navy, P1 red.
*8th row:* Knit, navy.
*9th row:* Purl, navy. Rep previous 4 rows 6 times, then 6th and 7th rows once.
*Next row:* (Navy) K8, K2 tog, K7, K2 tog, K16, K2 tog, K7, K2 tog, K8 (50 sts). Knit 4 rows. Cast off.

### To make up

Using tapestry needle and navy yarn, work from right side. Overcast first vertical navy rows together at side edges to conceal coloured st at beginning and end of rows. Turn bag to wrong side, fold in half with seam at centre back and sew cast-on edges together. Secure all remaining threads.

## PILLOW

Pick up 18 sts (9 either side of back seam) at top of bag on the inside. Knit 56 rows. Cast off. Fold in half and sew one side and cast-off edge to conceal first row of pillow. Insert small pieces of filling, sew remaining side.

# Cheeky the Clown

DESIGNED BY GWEN MERRILL

Make this lovable cheeky clown — choose the gayest, brightest fabrics you can find, and you will liven up any child's bedroom.

50 × 90 cm one-way stretch fabric for arms and body
two 34 × 14 cm pieces striped fabric for legs
40 × 90 cm fabric for smock
70 × 20 cm bias fabric and 70 cm ricrac for frill
45 × 90 cm printed fabric for pants
25 cm square pieces of red, black and white felt
1 m cord for laces
25 m 5-ply acrylic macrame cord and 30 cm cotton tape for hair
thick red yarn for pompon
matching sewing thread for body and felt
polyester fibre filling
1 m narrow elastic

All seams are sewn with right sides together unless otherwise indicated. 5 mm seam allowances are included on pattern pieces. Use stretch stitch when sewing stretch fabric.

## To make patterns

Enlarge clown body and clothing patterns (*see Fig. 1 pp. 30–31*) following the directions given on page 6.

## To make clown

**Shoe and leg:** Cut 2 complete shoe sections in white felt; 2 soles, 4 heel and 2 toe pieces in red felt; 2 pieces in black felt for tie section. For legs cut two, 34 × 14 cm pieces in striped cotton.

Topstitch heel, toe and tie section to white shoe shape. Topstitch shoe to right side of short side of leg piece from A to B. Pierce holes as marked and insert laces. With wrong sides together, sew back leg and shoe seam. Turn to right side, pin shoe to sole and topstitch around. Fill foot and halfway up leg. Stitch across knee, making sure back

*Cheeky the Clown*

seam is at centre. Fill top of leg, sew across.

**Body and arms:** Cut 2 pairs of body pieces, 2 arms on fold. Sew arms from E to F. Clip between fingers, turn to right side. Sew fingers as marked and across wrist, elbow and shoulder as each section is filled. Sew centre front and back body seams from C to D; then front and back head from shoulder (E) to shoulder. With arms inside the body and matching at E, sew side body seam. Turn to right side. Fill head and body. Turn in 5 mm at lower edge of body, insert legs and sew across.

**Hair:** (*See Fig. 2 page 30*). Place cord across tape making 7 cm loops alternately on each side of tape as shown. Sew by machine with matching thread along centre of tape across cord, securing each loop as it is made. Continue to end of tape pushing each loop firmly against previous loop. Turn and make another layer of loops on top of first layer in same way. Handsew tape to head at position marked with ends extending 3 cm on to face.

**Face:** Make a pompon, 5 cm diameter, for nose. Sew to face at centre. Cut mouth and cheeks in red felt, eyes and eyebrows in black felt. Handsew to face, following photograph.

**Smock:** Cut front, back, 2 sleeves, 70 × 20 cm bias fabric for frill. Sew sleeves to front and back at shoulder. Sew ends of frill together. Sew one edge of frill to neck, right sides together. Turn in seam allowance on remaining edge of frill and pin to wrong side neck. Sew close to edge leaving an opening for elastic. Sew second row 6 mm from first row of stitching for casing. Sew braid around edge. Sew underarm and side seams. Make 3 cm hem at wrist, sew 6 mm from stitching to make casing.

Insert elastic in neck and wrists. Hem smock bottom.

**Pants:** Cut 2 pieces on fold. Sew at centre back and front, then inside leg. Make a 6 mm casing at waist. Make casing and frill on leg as for wrist. Insert elastic in waist and legs.

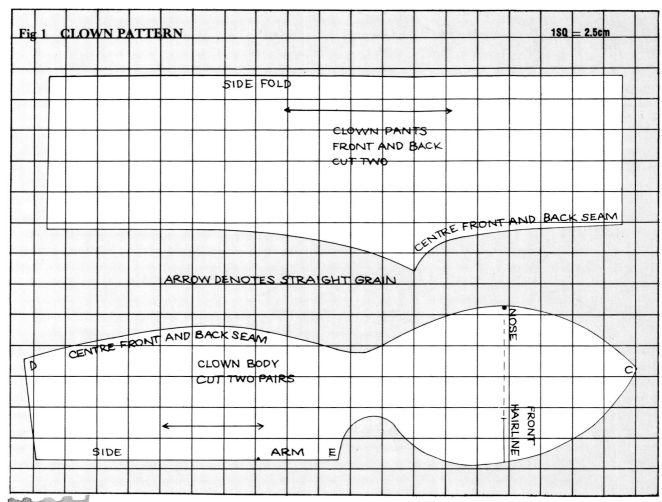

Fig 1  **CLOWN PATTERN**

1SQ = 2.5cm

SIDE FOLD

CLOWN PANTS
FRONT AND BACK
CUT TWO

CENTRE FRONT AND BACK SEAM

ARROW DENOTES STRAIGHT GRAIN

CENTRE FRONT AND BACK SEAM

CLOWN BODY
CUT TWO PAIRS

NOSE

FRONT HAIRLINE

D

C

SIDE

ARM

E

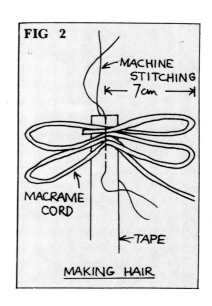

FIG 2

MACHINE
STITCHING

7cm

MACRAME
CORD

TAPE

MAKING HAIR

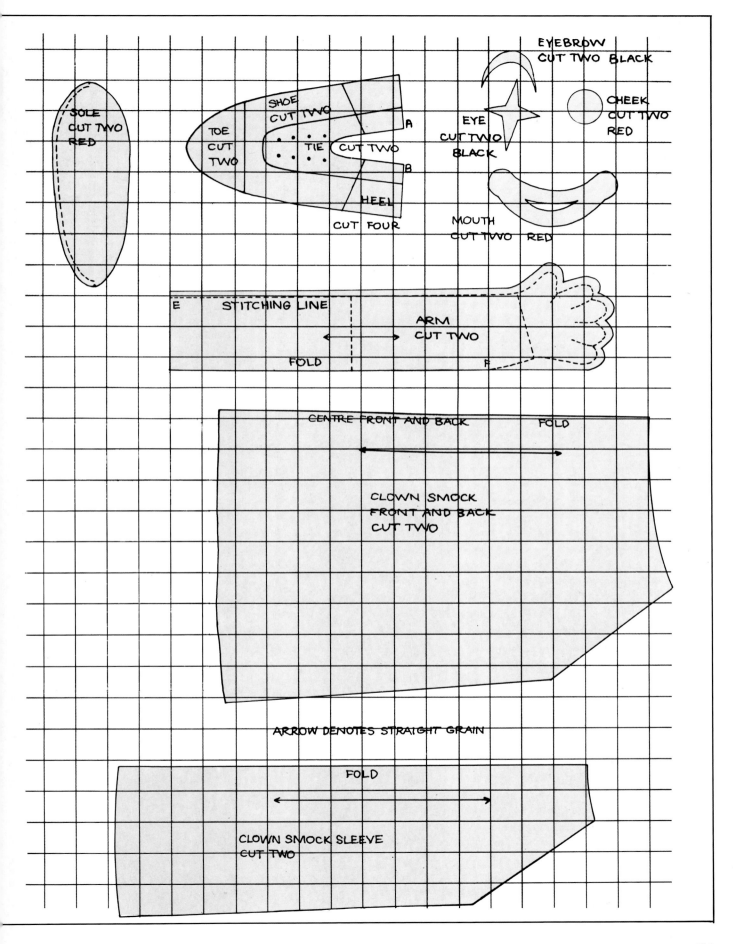

# Happy Families

Soft and cuddly farm animals make a happy family for the budding farmer in your life. Here are rabbits, large and small, sheep, lambs, hens and chicks to give you hours of fun.

*(large rabbits are about 71 cm high; small ones about 35.5 cm high)*

*(sheep measures about 53 cm long × 40 cm high; lamb 25 × 18 cm)*

*(hen measures 35 cm long × 28 cm high; chick, 18 × 12 cm)*

To make the patterns, follow directions **on page 6. Solid lines are cutting lines; broken ones, stitching or placement lines. See page 34 for patterns.**

When making patterns, copy and transfer all markings (stitching and placement lines, dart lines etc.). 1 cm seams are allowed throughout unless otherwise indicated. To cut 'one pair' (a front and back), cut on folded fabric.

After stitching, trim all seams to 5 cm and clip or notch curves.

To add body and eliminate fraying on appliqué, back pieces with iron-on interfacing. Trace pattern on to fabric, iron interfacing on to back of fabric, then cut out shape through both layers.

## RABBITS

Print or plush fabric at least 115 cm wide, 1 m for large rabbit, 50 cm for small
scraps of contrasting print fabrics for ear and paw appliqués
scraps of black, light pink and magenta felt for features
iron-on interfacing
white glue
1.25 m × 3.5 cm wide ribbon for large rabbit
70 cm × 2.5 cm wide ribbon for small rabbit
polyester fibre filling
4 ply yarn for tail

### To make rabbits

1. To cut rabbit body, fold each selvedge towards centre. Pin pattern along one fold, cut out front; repeat at other

*Rabbits, large and small, from the Happy Families collection*

fold to cut out back. Cut paw and ear appliqués, one pair of each.
2. Pin appliqués in place then zigzag around edges.
3. With right sides together, pin body front to back. Leaving an opening along one side of body for turning, stitch pieces together (5 mm seams on small rabbits), tapering seams to dots between ears and legs and at neck. Reinforce these points by stitching again. Slash up to seamline at inside corners. Turn body right side out.
4. Beginning with ears, stuff firmly to joint line; pin layers together along this line. Stuff and pin arms and legs in same way, stuff head and body. Slipstitch opening closed.
5. With double thread stitch along pinned lines; remove pins.
6. Cut out black felt eyes and mouth, pink cheeks and magenta nose; glue on.
7. *Pompon for tail:* For large rabbit cut two 7.5 cm cardboard circles with 2.5 cm hole in centre. For small rabbit cut two 5 cm circles with 2 cm holes. Hold circles together and wind yarn around and around until hole is almost filled in; cut yarn end. Insert scissors between cardboard circles and cut yarn all around. Tie a 25 cm length of yarn around centre of yarn, bundle between circles and tie tightly. Remove cardboard, trim pompon evenly. Sew to back of rabbit.
8. Tie a ribbon bow around neck.

## SHEEP AND LAMB

*For sheep:* 115 cm or wider fabric × 50 cm white plush and 25 cm dark blue print (for face and feet)
scraps of light blue fabric for legs and ear facings
*For lamb:* 20.5 cm × 30.5 cm piece of white plush
scraps of dark and light blue print fabrics
*For sheep and lamb:* Scrap of black felt for features

polyester fibre filling
1 m × 3.5 cm wide ribbon for sheep
50 cm × 2.5 cm wide ribbon for lamb
white glue

### To make sheep

1. From plush, cut a body, a pair of head/neck sections, a pair of ears and one 9 × 13 cm strip for tail; from dark print, cut a pair of faces and four pairs of feet; from light print cut a pair of ear facings and legs.
2. Fold tail in half lengthwise with right sides together; stitch along side and one end. Turn to right side.
3. Pin tail to right side of body between circles, matching raw edges; baste across tail end. Fold body right sides together and edges matching. Stitch, leaving opening at neck edge (beyond dot) for turning. Turn right side out. Stuff firmly and pin closed temporarily.
4. With right sides together, pin one face to each head/neck along edge B; stitch, clipping curve. Set aside.
5. Stitch an ear to each ear facing, with right sides together, leaving straight end open. Turn right side out and press. At the opening turn raw edges to inside and slipstitch closed. Stitch an ear to each head/neck, between circles.
6. With right sides facing stitch head sections together, leaving neck edge open (take care not to catch ears in seam). Turn right side out. Stuff head firmly all the way to neck opening.
7. Remove pins and turn under neck opening edges of body 1 cm; insert head 2.5 cm into body, pin. With double thread, sew neck opening to head securely.
8. For legs, with right sides together, stitch top of each foot to bottom of a leg section along edges A; repeat until you have eight pieces. Press seams open. Then, with right sides facing, stitch pairs of feet and leg pieces together, leaving tops open. Turn legs right side out. Stuff firmly to top, turn top edges 1 cm to inside and slipstitch together. Handsew legs to body where indicated.
9. From felt, cut mouth and eyelashes. Glue in place, curving mouth into a smile and curving eyelashes slightly. Tie neck bow.

### Lamb

Make same as sheep using 5 mm seams. Cut tail 4.5 × 6.5 cm, ears from dark print and head and neck section from light print.

*Hen and chicks*

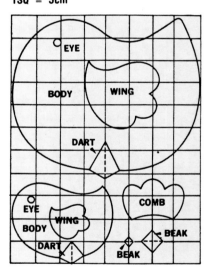

*Sheep and lamb*

# HEN AND CHICKS

*For hen:* print fabrics 50 × 115 cm wide for body and 15 × 35.5 cm piece for wings

scrap of red print fabric for comb

*For each chick:* 20 × 46 cm print or yellow plush fabric for body

scrap of print for wings

*For all:* scraps of orange and black felt

polyester fibre filling

white glue

iron-on interfacing

## To make hen

1. From print, cut one pair each of body, wing appliqué and comb pieces.
2. Pin wings to body pieces, zigzag around wing edges.
3. Stitch darts in bodies, press.
4. With right sides together, stitch 5 mm seam on comb pieces, leaving bottom open. Clip at inside corners. Turn right side out. Stuff lightly, stitch bottom.

5. Pin comb to outside of one body piece, matching raw edges between circles clipping curve, baste. With right sides facing, pin body together; stitch, leaving opening for turning. Turn to right side. Stuff, slipstitch opening.

6. Cut out black eyes and orange beak. Handsew beak in place through centre; glue eyes in place.

## Chicks

Make as hen. Omit comb.

**FIG 1    RABBITS      1SQ = 5cm**
**for large rabbit**

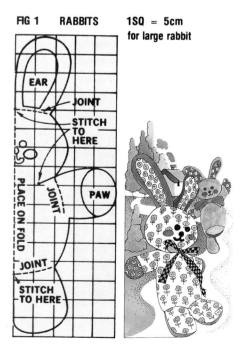

**FIG 2    LAMBS      1SQ = 2.5cm**

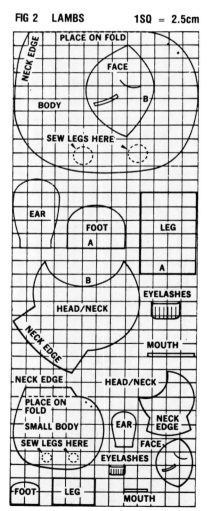

**FIG 3    CHICKENS**
**1SQ = 5cm**

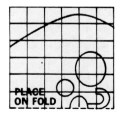

**1SQ = 2.5cm**
**for small rabbit**

**1SQ = 1.2cm**
**for small rabbit face**

# Russian Dolls in Tapestry

These pretty Russian mother and daughter dolls are made up in colourfully embroidered canvas. You can expand the family by adding more daughters, if you like.

Coats Anchor Tapisserie Wool: 1 skein each Moss Green 0268, Amber Gold 0305, Tangerine 0313, Orange 0325, Flame 0334, Chestnut 0347, Coffee 0381, White 0402, Black 0403, Gold 0500, Spice Brown 0570, Sage Green 0845, Pink 0896 and Smoke 0985
*Alternative thread:* Anchor Stranded Cotton: 3 skeins Raspberry 069, Black 0403, 2 skeins each Muscat Green 0281, Tangerine 0311, Cinnamon 0366, 1 skein each Moss Green 0268, Buttercup 0292, Amber Gold 0305, Orange 0324, Flame 0333, Peat Brown 0359, Linen 0393 and White 0402, use 9 strands throughout
Anchor Embroidery Canvas Pack Art No. HS 0902 or 30 cm double thread tapestry canvas, 10 holes to 2.5 cm, 68 cm wide
1 piece wine backing fabric 30 × 20 cm for Mother Doll and 1 piece dark brown backing fabric 20 × 16 cm for Daughter Doll
polyester fibre filling
small piece of thick cardboard for base 12 × 10 cm
tapestry frame with 46 cm tapes
Milward International Range tapestry needle No. 18

## To make dolls

Cut two pieces from canvas 30 × 30 cm. Mark the centre of each piece with a line of basting stitches run between a pair of narrow threads lengthwise and along a line of holes widthwise. Mount one piece of canvas in frame. The diagrams on page 37 give one half of each doll (*Mother, Fig. 1; Daughter, Fig. 2, p. 37*), centres indicated by the arrows which should coincide with the basting stitches. Each background square on the diagrams represents the double threads of the canvas. The design is worked throughout in trammed gros point stitch (*see diagrams p. 6*). Commence Mother Doll centrally and work given half following diagram and key (*see Fig. 3 on page 37*) for embroidery. To complete, work other half in reverse. Work Daughter Doll in the same way.

## To make up

Trim canvas to within 1.5 cm of embroidery. Cut backing fabric to same size. Place canvas and backing fabric right sides together, then baste and stitch close to embroidery leaving lower edge open. Trim seams and press open. Turn to right side. Turn in seam allowance at lower edge to wrong side. Stuff firmly. From cardboard cut one piece 9.5 × 3.5 cm and one piece 7 × 2.5 cm for base of dolls. Round off the corners of each piece to fit. Cut fabric 1 cm larger all round. Work a row of running stitches 5 mm from edge of fabric then place cardboard centrally and draw thread up tightly. Place base in position and oversew.

## Russian Dolls in Tapestry

Follow our colour chart key at right (see Fig. 3)

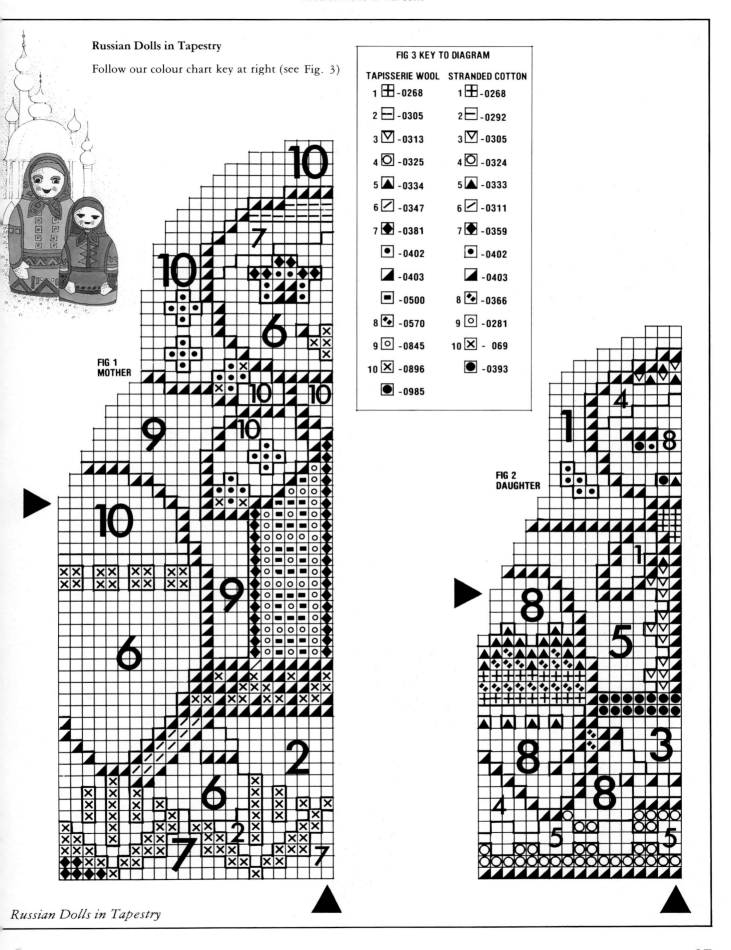

**FIG 3 KEY TO DIAGRAM**

| TAPISSERIE WOOL | STRANDED COTTON |
|---|---|
| 1 ⊞ -0268 | 1 ⊞ -0268 |
| 2 ⊟ -0305 | 2 ⊟ -0292 |
| 3 ▽ -0313 | 3 ▽ -0305 |
| 4 ◯ -0325 | 4 ◯ -0324 |
| 5 ▲ -0334 | 5 ▲ -0333 |
| 6 ◿ -0347 | 6 ◿ -0311 |
| 7 ◆ -0381 | 7 ◆ -0359 |
| ⊙ -0402 | ⊙ -0402 |
| ◢ -0403 | ◢ -0403 |
| ▬ -0500 | 8 ◈ -0366 |
| 8 ◈ -0570 | 9 ⊡ -0281 |
| 9 ⊡ -0845 | 10 ✕ - 069 |
| 10 ✕ -0896 | ● -0393 |
| ● -0985 | |

**FIG 1 MOTHER**

**FIG 2 DAUGHTER**

# Pretty Polly

DESIGNED BY GWEN MERRILL

A lovable calico doll and her outfit. Polly stands 58 cm tall.

## DOLL

60 cm of 90 cm-wide calico
one 50 g ball Sirdar Pullman 12-ply
   yarn
scraps black, brown and white felt
black embroidery thread
polyester fibre filling
six small two-hole buttons
strong thread
1 m ribbon
red pencil and brown felt pen for
   features

1. Following instructions on page 6 enlarge all diagrams in Fig. 1 (p. 41). Use 5 mm seams.
2. From calico cut pattern pieces for doll body. Cut out eye pieces in felt.
3. *Hair*: Wind all yarn around a book (20 cm wide × 1 cm thick), cut yarn along spine of book and divide in half. Slash head gusset from A to C, machine stitch ends of one half of hair to edge of slash on right side of gusset between B and C. Repeat for other side of slash. Fold gusset in half (with hair inside) and sew from A tapering to nothing 1 cm past C.
4. Sew two ear pieces together round curved edge, turn, fill softly and sew across straight edge. Repeat for other ear. Sew ears to front side heads, sew front and back side heads together. Beginning at front neck sew side heads to head gusset. Sew dart at chin. Turn to right side.
5. Sew darts on back body. Sew front to back body from D to E.
6. Insert head inside body with right sides together. Matching side seams sew neckline.
7. Sew around arms, turn, sew fingers then fill firmly. Fill arm softly, slip-stitch opening. Sew arm to body, stitching through three buttons: placed inside body, between arm and body and on outside of arm.
8. Fill head, neck, shoulders and body firmly. Turn in seam allowance across bottom of body.
9. Clip seam allowance of inner curve

*Pretty Polly — dress, apron and shoes*

of foot then sew to leg. Fold in half, right sides together, and sew back seam. Gather front of foot, sew sole to foot. Fill firmly to within 2 cm from top, sew across with seam at centre back. Insert legs into body, handsew across front and back inserting more filling if necessary.
10. Secure hair at ear with a couple of stitches, divide hair into three and plait. Secure ends in rubber bands and tie with ribbon. Cut a few strands at front for fringe.
11. Assemble felt eye pieces following Fig. 2. Using black, sew black and brown felt to white with straight stitches. Sew eye to face with white. Work 2 rows black backstitch across top and corners of eye, work straight stitches for lashes.
12. Colour cheeks with red pencil, draw nose, mouth and freckles in brown.

## DOLL'S CLOTHES

Following the instructions on page 6 enlarge the diagrams in Figs. 3–5 (pp. 42–3). A 5 mm seam allowance is included on pattern. Neaten all raw edges.

## DRESS
### (Fig. 3)

30 cm each of 90 cm-wide plain and
   patterned fabric
1.2 m lace
five press-studs
bias strip
narrow elastic

1. From plain fabric cut front and back bodice plus a 15 × 80 cm strip for skirt. In contrast fabric cut sleeves, collars, 3.5 × 36 cm strip for waistband; sufficient 8 cm-wide strips to make a 120 cm strip for frill.
2. Sew shoulder seams. Sew collars round curved edge, clip seam, turn and press. Baste to neck with collars meeting at centre front and back. Neaten back raw edges, turn facings to right side—overlapping edge of collar. With right sides to collar sew bias strip to

neck seamline, clip, fold over seam allowance and slipstitch to bodice.
3. Gather top of sleeves. Sew to armhole, sew underarm and side seam. Make a 2 cm hem at cuff, sew 7 mm from hem machining, leaving a small gap. Insert and secure elastic.
4. Sew waistband to bodice. Join frill pieces to make 120 cm, sew lace to one long edge, gather other edge and sew to long edge of skirt. Gather top edge of skirt and sew to waistband. Neaten back edge and turn under facing. Sew press-studs to back opening.

## APRON

20 cm of 90 cm-wide gingham fabric
two 6 × 5 cm pieces plain fabric for
   pockets
1.2 m lace
12 mm button
two press-studs

1. Cut waistband 5 × 36 cm, two shoulder straps 5 × 24 cm, two bibs 8 cm square, one skirt 15 × 30 cm.
2. Gather 40 cm lace and sew to two sides and top of one bib. Fold strap right sides together and sew one long side and across one end, turn to right side. Baste and sew bib facing to right side bib with straps inserted in seamline at top. Leave waist open, turn to right side.
3. Press 5 mm hem around all sides of pockets, sew to skirt. Gather lace and sew to sides and bottom of skirt. Gather waist to measure 16 cm. With centres matching and wrong sides together, baste bib to skirt then with right sides together baste waistband to skirt. Sew through all layers.
4. Fold waistband in half, sew from edge of skirt across ends, pull through to right side. Hem waistband across skirt, make buttonhole and sew button to waistband ends.
5. With apron on doll cross straps at back and sew press-studs as required.

## BLOOMERS
### (Fig. 4)

20 × 50 cm fabric
narrow elastic

1. Cut two front and back pieces.
2. Sew centre front and back seams. Turn under and sew a 2 cm hem round legs, sew 7 mm from machining to make casing, leaving gap. Turn under 1 cm round waist and machine stitch, leaving opening. Insert elastic in leg casings and waist.

*Skirt, blouse, headscarf and shoes*

# TAN/BROWN SHOES
*(Fig. 7)*

24 cm square tan felt
14 × 12 cm brown felt
40 cm cord

1. Cut two shoe uppers and soles in tan, two brown trims.
2. Beginning at back edgestitch trim to shoe upper on right side. Sew circle on extensions, pierce holes.
3. Gather between dots. Sew back seam, edgestitch allowance. With right sides inside, sew upper to sole, easing toe as you sew with centre front and back matching, turn to right side. Thread tie and knot ends.

# BLOUSE
*(Fig. 5)*

30 cm of 90 cm wide fabric
60 cm narrow braid
three press-studs
narrow elastic

1. Cut one front, two backs and two sleeves.
2. Sew sleeves to front and back. Turn under facings at back opening. Gather neck to 20 cm, machine stitch gathers, sew braid to conceal raw edge.

3. Sew underarm and side seams. Make a 2.5 cm hem at cuffs, sew 7 mm from hem machining to make casement leaving a gap. Sew braid to cuff edge, insert elastic in casing.
4. Make a narrow hem round edge of blouse, sew press-studs to back.

# TIERED SKIRT
*(length 24 cm)*

One 9 × 38 cm piece fabric for top tier
one 15 × 80 cm for middle tier
one 6 × 80 cm for bottom tier
80 cm of 2 cm lace
narrow elastic

1. With right sides facing sew lace to bottom tier. Sew bottom tier to middle tier, make a 1.5 cm-wide tuck at seamline. Gather top of middle tier to 38 cm, sew to top tier. Sew back seam.
2. Make a 1 cm hem round waist, insert elastic.

# HEADSCARF

Cut a triangle measuring 38 × 38 × 54 cm. Machine hem all three sides.

# TRACKSUIT
*(Fig. 6)*

70 cm of 115 cm-wide stretch velour
2.4 m of 1 cm-wide braid
1.2 m narrow elastic

1. Cut one back, two fronts, two sleeves, too hood pieces and two trouser legs.
2. **Pants:** Sew braid down side leg. Sew front and back seams, then inner leg seams. Turn under 12 mm at waist and cuffs, zigzag over raw edge leaving an opening, insert elastic.
3. **Jacket:** Sew braid to sleeve, sew hood pieces together round curved edge. Sew sleeves to back and front. Sew hood to neck. Sew fronts together to A with a 12 mm seam allowance. Press seam allowance flat, turn under 12 mm around front opening and hood. Sew braid around front opening and hood.
4. Cut two 30 cm ties and sew to neck. Turn under 12 mm at waist and wrist, zigzag leaving a gap, insert elastic.

# BLACK SHOES
*(Fig. 8)*

24 cm square black felt
1 m of 3 mm-wide cord braid

two 10 mm shank buttons
1. Cut two shoe uppers, two soles.
2. Cut strap at edge of shoe on one side only. Starting at back sew braid to right side of shoe edge continuing it at strap end to form button loop. Reverse strap opening on other shoe.
3. Follow directions for **Tan/Brown shoes** from * to * Sew buttons.

# SNEAKERS
*(Fig. 9)*

20 × 25 cm navy felt
15 × 20 cm white felt
70 cm braid
eight eyelets

1. In navy cut two soles, two toes, two trims, eight stripes. In white cut two uppers (complete shape).
2. Position stripes to upper as marked and sew. Sew trim to top edge of upper covering stripes.
3. Bring points A together, catchstitch. Overlap toe 5 mm on to upper and topstitch. Gather between dots.
4. With right sides inside, sew upper to sole easing toe into sole, turn. Attach eyelets, thread laces.

*Tracksuit and sneakers*

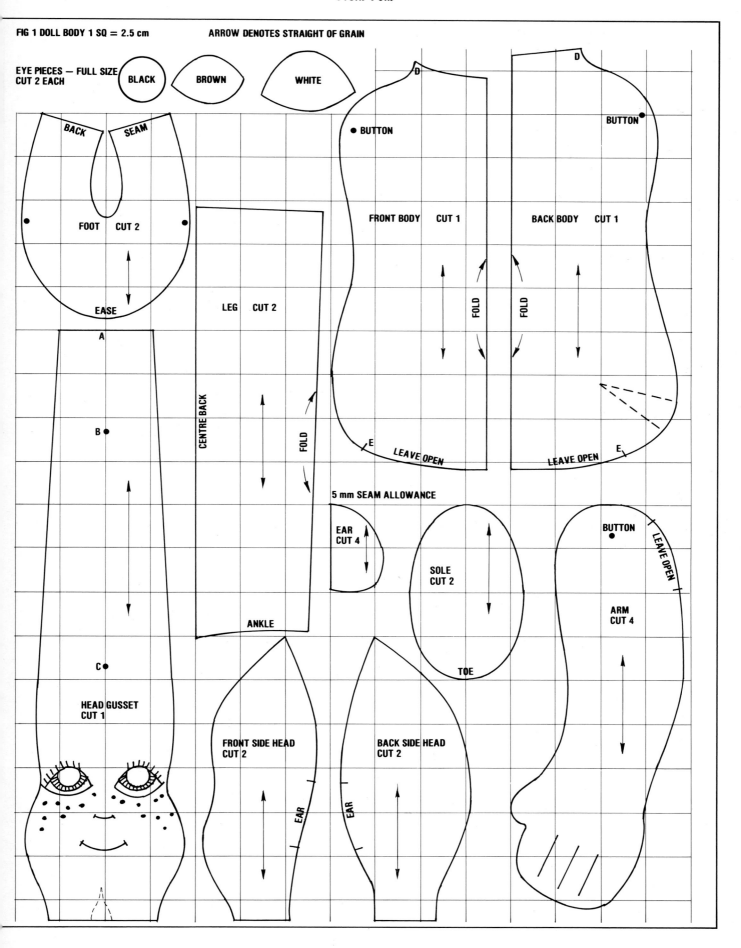

FIG 1 DOLL BODY 1 SQ = 2.5 cm    ARROW DENOTES STRAIGHT OF GRAIN

EYE PIECES — FULL SIZE
CUT 2 EACH    BLACK    BROWN    WHITE

BACK SEAM

FOOT    CUT 2

EASE

A

B

C

HEAD GUSSET
CUT 1

LEG    CUT 2

CENTRE BACK

FOLD

ANKLE

5 mm SEAM ALLOWANCE

EAR
CUT 4

FRONT SIDE HEAD
CUT 2

EAR

BACK SIDE HEAD
CUT 2

EAR

BUTTON

FRONT BODY    CUT 1

FOLD    FOLD

E    LEAVE OPEN

D

BUTTON

BACK BODY    CUT 1

FOLD

LEAVE OPEN    E

SOLE
CUT 2

TOE

BUTTON

LEAVE OPEN

ARM
CUT 4

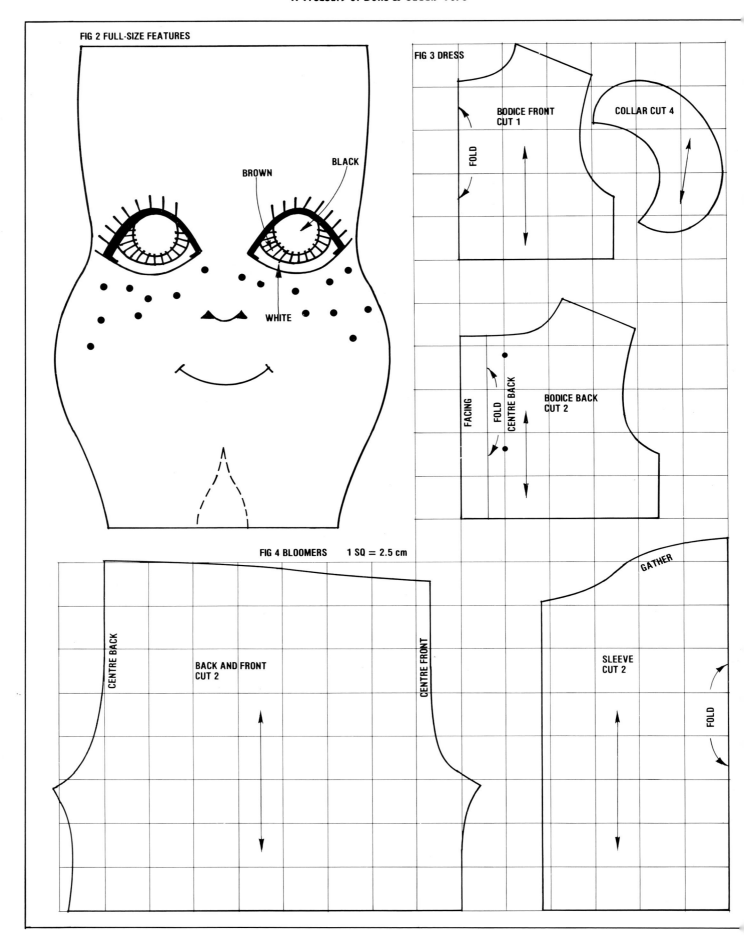

FIG 2 FULL-SIZE FEATURES

BROWN

BLACK

WHITE

FIG 3 DRESS

BODICE FRONT CUT 1

FOLD

COLLAR CUT 4

FACING

FOLD

CENTRE BACK

BODICE BACK CUT 2

FIG 4 BLOOMERS    1 SQ = 2.5 cm

CENTRE BACK

BACK AND FRONT CUT 2

CENTRE FRONT

GATHER

SLEEVE CUT 2

FOLD

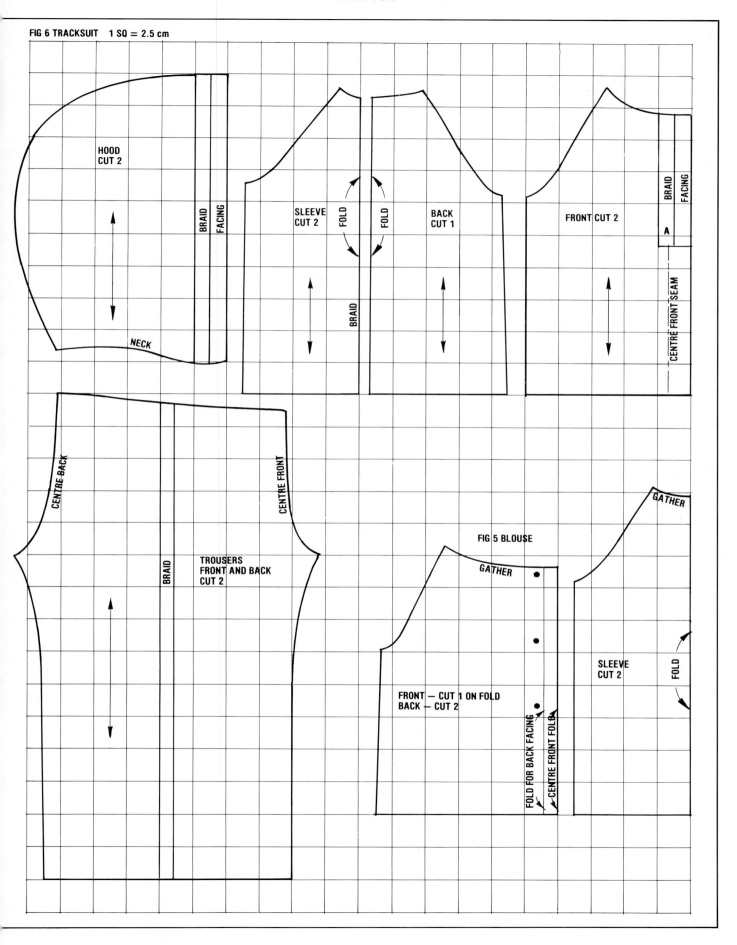

FIG 6 TRACKSUIT   1 SQ = 2.5 cm

HOOD CUT 2

BRAID

FACING

NECK

SLEEVE CUT 2

FOLD

FOLD

BRAID

BACK CUT 1

FRONT CUT 2

BRAID

FACING

A

CENTRE FRONT SEAM

CENTRE BACK

CENTRE FRONT

BRAID

TROUSERS FRONT AND BACK CUT 2

FIG 5 BLOUSE

GATHER

GATHER

FRONT — CUT 1 ON FOLD
BACK — CUT 2

FOLD FOR BACK FACING

CENTRE FRONT FOLD

SLEEVE CUT 2

FOLD

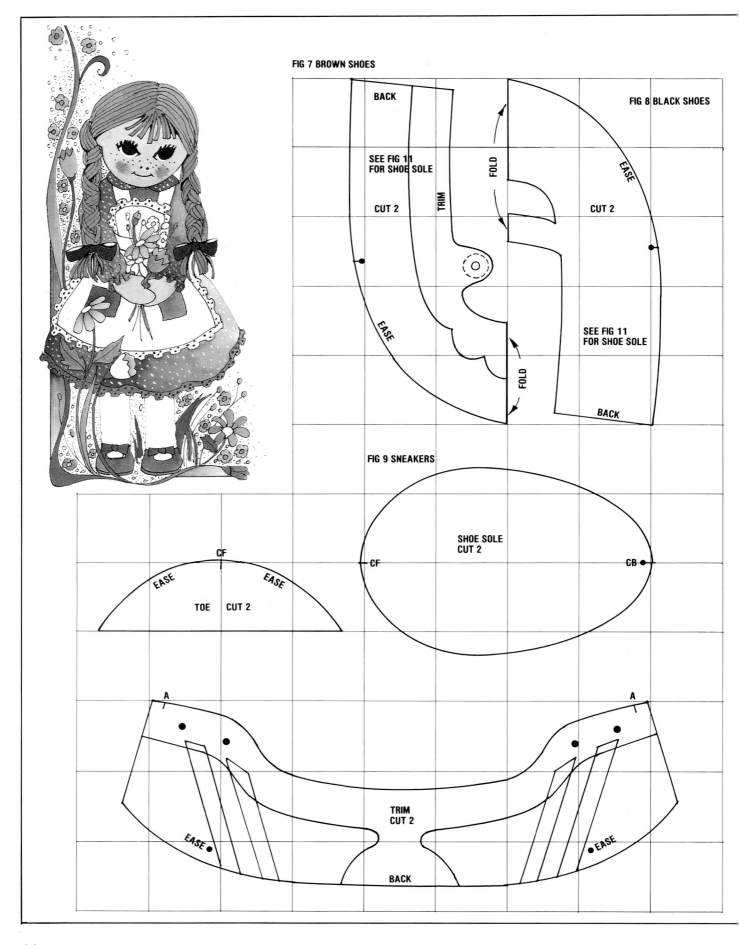

FIG 7 BROWN SHOES

BACK

FIG 8 BLACK SHOES

SEE FIG 11
FOR SHOE SOLE

CUT 2

FOLD

EASE

TRIM

CUT 2

EASE

SEE FIG 11
FOR SHOE SOLE

FOLD

BACK

FIG 9 SNEAKERS

SHOE SOLE
CUT 2

CF — CF — CB ●

EASE    EASE

TOE    CUT 2

A                    A

TRIM
CUT 2

EASE ●                    ● EASE

BACK

# Crochet Sheep to Cuddle

DESIGNED BY GWEN MERRILL

A family of four sheep: Baby 12 cm high, Junior 14 cm, Mum 16 cm, and Dad 19 cm.

*Crochet Sheep to Cuddle (see title page for full family)*

Sirdar Pullman 12-ply in ivory (50 g balls)—1 Baby, 2 Junior, 3 Mum, 4 Dad
1 ball of black sufficient for 4 sheep
1 pr 10 mm plastic animal eyes for each sheep
5.00 mm (No. 6) crochet hook
tapestry needle
polyester fibre filling
*Tension:* 4 sts to 3.5 cm in width over loop stitch; 4 sts to 3 cm in width over double crochet.
*Abbreviations:* dc — *double crochet*; ch — *chain*; st(s) — *stitch(es)*; lp st(s) — *loop stitch(es)*; inc — *increase*; rem — *remaining*; sl st — *slip stitch*; rnd(s) — *round(s)*; beg — *beginning*; patt — *pattern*.

## To make sheep

Body is crocheted in rounds of loop stitch beginning at tail. Face, legs, ears and horns are worked in double crochet and added separately.
*Loop stitch*: **See p. 7 for how to work** loop stitch. Loops are formed on back of work. For Baby hold finger close to work when forming loops; for Dad extend finger for larger loops. The rounds for body are worked with loops on inside of body.

## Body

**Baby:** Using 5.00 mm crochet hook and ivory, ch 2, work 3 lp sts into first ch. Work 2 lp sts into each st in the next 3 rnds until 24 sts *. Work 12 rnds without shaping leaving sufficient wool to complete 2 rnds.
*Shape neck:* Dec 2 sts at the beg on next 2 rnds, sl 1, fasten off. Tie markers at centre of shaping to position head and mark centre of underbody.
**Junior:** Work to * for Baby (24 sts).
*5th rnd:* Inc in every 4th st around (30 sts). Work 17 rnds.
*Shape neck:* Dec 2 sts at same place in next 3 rnds until 24 sts rem, sl 1, fasten off. With a new thread work 6 lp sts across top of head opposite decreasing rows, sl 1 fasten off.
**Mum:** Work to * for Baby (24 sts).
*5th rnd:* Inc in every other st around (36 sts). Work 21 rnds.
*Shape neck:* Dec 2 sts at same place in next 5 rnds until 26 sts rem, sl 1, fasten off. With a new thread work 8 lp sts across top of head opposite decreasing rows, sl 1, fasten off.
**Dad:** Work to 5th rnd for Mum (36 sts).
*6th rnd:* Inc in every 4th st around (45 sts). Work 24 rnds.
*Shape neck:* Dec 3 sts, at same place in next 5 rnds until 30 sts rem. With a new thread work 12 lp sts across top of head opposite decreasing rows, sl 1, fasten off.

## Legs (make 4)

Using black and 5.00 mm crochet hook, ch 2. Work 5 dc (Baby and Junior), 6 dc (Mum and Dad) into first ch. Cont working in rnds for 5, 6, 7 or 8 rnds respectively. Sl 1, fasten off. Leave end long enough for sewing leg to body.

## Face

**Baby:** Using black and 5.00 mm crochet hook ch 2. Work 4 dc in first ch.
*Next rnd:* Inc in every st around (8 dc). Work 1 rnd.
*Next rnd:* Inc in every other dc around (12 dc) *. Work 1 rnd.
*Next rnd:* Inc in every other dc around (18 dc). Work 1 rnd.
*Next rnd:* Inc in next and 9th dc (20 dc). Complete rnd. Sl 1, fasten off.
**Junior:** Work to * for Baby (12 dc). Work 2 rnds.
*Next rnd:* Inc in every other dc around (18 dc). Work 1 rnd.
*Next rnd:* Inc in every 3rd st around (24 dc). Work 1 rnd. Sl 1, fasten off.
**Mum:** 2 ch, 8 dc in first ch.
*Next rnd:* Inc in every other dc around (12 dc). Work 1 rnd.
*Next rnd:* Inc in every 4th dc around (15 dc). Work 3 rnds.
*Next rnd:* Inc in every 3rd dc around (20 dc). Work 1 rnd. *
*Next rnd:* Inc 6 dc evenly around (26 dc). Work 1 rnd, sl 1, fasten off.
**Dad:** Work to * for Mum (20 dc).
*Next rnd:* Inc in every other dc around (30 dc). Work 4 rounds, sl 1, fasten off.

## Ear (make 2)

**Baby and Junior:** 7 ch, sl 1, into 2nd ch from hook, 1 dc, miss 2 dc, 1 dc sl 1, do not ch to turn.
*Next row:* Miss 2 dc, sl 1, fasten off.
**Mum and Dad:** 11 ch, 1 dc into 2nd ch from hook, 3 dc, miss 2 ch, 4 dc, do not ch to turn.
*Next row:* Miss 1 st, sl 1, 1 dc, miss 2 dc, 1 dc, miss 1, sl 1, do not ch to turn.
*Next row:* Miss 1 st, sl 1, miss 1, sl 1, fasten off.

## Horn

*Left side:* Using ivory ch 8, sl st in first ch to form circle. Work 16 rnds in dc, dec one st at the beg of 4th, 7th, 10th, 13th and 16th rnds, use markers to keep dec even. Work 3 rnds, miss 1, sl 1. Fasten off, leaving end long enough to sew back along the horn.
*Note:* For right side horn to curve in opposite direction, work 4 rnds, turn horn inside out and complete following instructions for left side.

Using tapestry needle and wool hand sew any holes in work at tip of horn, weave back along line of dec to beg of work.

Fill each horn firmly with small pieces of fibre. Pull up gathering thread to curve for left or right side of head, fasten off.

## To make up

Sew holes at beg of legs and fill firmly with scraps of black wool. Sew legs to under body 4 sts apart at front and back. Fill body softly. Sew hole at end of nose. Turn face inside out for better shape. Insert plastic eyes and check placement before attaching metal back. Fill firmly with scraps of black wool. Sew face to body inserting more filling if necessary. Sew ears to face above eyes to curve forward. Sew horns to body behind ears.

# Blackfaced Sheep to Knit

DESIGNED BY GWEN MERRILL

These lovable blackfaced sheep have rainbow coloured garments and furry mohair heads. You can add decorations to their clothing, with bright buttons in the shape of alphabet letters, hearts and other exciting shapes. They are about 35 mm tall.

Small quantities of Patons Totem 8-ply wool or yarn in green, red, blue, navy, yellow, emerald and black

small quantity heavy gauge mohair bouclé yarn (approximately 20-ply)—available from most craft shops

three 3.25 mm (No. 10) and one pair 4.5 mm (No. 7) knitting needles

1 pair 12 mm animal safety eyes for each sheep

tapestry needle

polyester fibre for filling

heart and alphabet button motifs

The legs and body are knitted in one piece commencing at the feet. Head and arms are worked separately. The girl's skirt is knitted in at the waist.

*Tension*: 8-ply—8 sts to 3 cm in width over st st using 3.25 mm needles. Bouclé—if a finer bouclé yarn is substituted do not decrease sts for arm and leg at wrist and ankle. Extra sts will need to be cast on for head and reduced in final rows to number required before working black face.

*Abbreviations:* K — *Knit*; P — *Purl*; st(s) — *stitch(es)*; cont — *continue*; tog — *together*; st st — *stocking stitch*; inc — *increase*; dec — *decrease*; sl st — *slip stitch*; alt — *alternate*; beg — *beginning*; foll — *following*; rep — *repeat*; yfwd — *yarn forward*; ybk — *yarn back*; make 1 — *pick up loop between sts on left hand needle and knit into back of loop.*

## BOY

**First leg** (*foot*): *Using 3.25 mm needles and black, cast on 8 sts.
*1st row:* Knit.
*2nd row:* Purl.
*3rd row:* Inc in first st, K2, make 1, K1, make 1, K3, inc in last st (12 sts).
*4th and alt rows:* Purl.
*5th row:* Inc in first st, K4, make 1, K1, make 1, K5, inc in last st (16 sts).
*7th row:* Inc in first st, K6, make 1, K1, make 1, K7, inc in last st (20 sts).
*9th row:* Inc in first st, K8, make 1, K1, make 1, K4, make 1, K1, make 1, K4, inc in last st (26 sts).
*11th row:* K18, make 1, K1, make 1, K7 (28 sts).
*13th row:* K19, make 1, K1, make 1, K8 (30 sts).**
*14th row:* P18, ybk, sl 1, turn, ybk, sl 1, K16, yfwd, sl 1, turn, yfwd, sl 1, P to end of row (30 sts).
Stocking stitch 2 rows. Break off black.
**Leg:** Join in bouclé, do not change needles.
*Next row:* (K2 tog, K2) 7 times, K2 tog (22 sts).***
Knit 3 rows. Break off yarn leave sts on needle.
**Cuff:** Using 3.25 mm needles and blue, cast on 30 sts. Knit 4 rows.
*Next row:* (K2 tog, K2) 7 times, K2 tog (22 sts).
*Join cuff to leg:* Hold leg (bouclé) with cuff at front in left hand. Knit together one st from each needle (22 sts).
Stocking stitch 29 rows.****
Break off yarn, leave sts on needle.

**Second leg:** Work from * to ** of first leg in *reverse*.
*14th row:* P28, ybk, sl 1, turn, ybk, sl 1, K16, yfwd, sl 1, turn, yfwd, sl 1, P to end of row (30 sts).

Stocking stitch 2 rows. Break off black. Continue following directions for first leg to ****.
**Join legs:** K11, make 1, K10, make 1, K1 (*second leg*) K1, make 1, K10, make 1, K11 (48 sts).
Stocking stitch 19 rows.
**Belt:** Join in navy. Knit 4 rows.
**Jumper:** Stocking stitch 10 rows red, 3 rows navy, 6 rows green, 3 rows navy, 2 rows red.
**Shape shoulders:** K11, K2 tog, K22, K2 tog, K11 (46 sts).
*Next and alt rows:* Purl.
*Next row:* K11, K2 tog, K20, K11 (44 sts). Cont to dec in same manner until 40 sts rem. Purl one row.
*Next row:* K1, (K2 tog, K2) 9 times, K2 tog, K1 (30 sts). Cast off.
**Roll neck collar:** Pick up 28 sts in red at neck. Knit 10 rows. Cast off loosely.
**Arm** (*Make two*): *Using 3.25 mm needles, cast on 8 sts in black. Purl one row.
*Next row:* (K1, make 1) 7 times, inc in last st (16 sts).
Cont in stocking stitch for 7 rows. Break off black.
*Next row:* Join in bouclé, K1 (K2 tog, K2) 3 times, K2 tog, K1 (12 sts). Knit 2 rows.
*Next row:* K1, make 1, K3, make 1, K4, make 1, K3, make 1, K1 (16 sts). Break off yarn leave sts on needle.

**Cuff:** Using 3.25 mm needles, cast on 20 sts in red. Knit 2 rows.
*Next row:* (K2 tog, K4) 3 times, K2 tog (16 sts).
*Join cuff to arm:* Hold arm (bouclé) with cuff at front in left hand. Knit together one st from each needle (16 sts)**.
Work 21 rows stocking stitch, inc one st each end of row in foll 7th, 11th, and 15th rows (22 sts). Commence 12 rows

of stripes as for jumper at 13th row.
*23rd and 24th rows:* (navy) Cast off 3 sts at beg of each row (16 sts).
Change to red and cast off 2 sts at beg of next 4 rows (8 sts).
Cast off.

**Head** *(Boy and Girl):* Using 4.5 mm needles and bouclé, cast on 10 sts.
*1st row:* Knit.
*2nd row:* Inc in each st (20 sts).
*3rd row:* Knit.
*4th row:* Inc in each st (40 sts).
Knit 13 rows. Break off yarn.

**Face:** Change to 3.25 mm needles and black.
*1st row:* K1 (K2 tog, K4) 6 times, K2 tog, K1 (33 sts).
Stocking stitch 3 rows.
*5th row:* (K2 tog, K3) 6 times, K2 tog, K1 (26 sts).
Stocking stitch 3 rows.
*9th row:* K2 tog, K5, K2 tog twice, K4, K2 tog twice, K5, K2 tog (20 sts).
Stocking stitch 3 rows.
*13th row:* K2 tog, K16, K2 tog (18 sts).
*14th row:* Purl.

*15th row:* (K2 tog, K1) 6 times (12 sts).
*16th row:* Purl.
Cast off.

**Ears** *(Make 2):* Using 3.25 mm needles and black cast on 6 sts.
Knit 4 rows.
*Next row:* K2 tog, K2, K2 tog (4 sts).
Knit 3 rows.
*Next row:* K2 tog twice.
*Next row:* K2 tog, fasten off.

# GIRL

**First leg:** Follow directions for Boy from * to ***.
Knit 5 rows. Break off bouclé.
Stocking stitch 28 rows, alternating 2 rows red and 2 rows white. Break off yarn, leave sts on needle.

**Second leg:** Follow directions for Boy first leg from * to ** in *reverse*.
*14th row:* P28, ybk, sl 1, turn, ybk, sl 1, K16, yfwd, sl 1, turn, yfwd, sl 1, P to end of row (30 sts).
Stocking stitch 2 rows. Break off black. Join in bouclé.
Complete to correspond with first leg.
Do not break off yarn.

**Join legs:** K11, make 1, K10, make 1, K1 *(second leg)* K1, make 1, K10, make 1, K11 (48 sts).

Stocking stitch 21 rows keeping stripes correct. Leave sts on needle.

**Skirt:** Using 3.25 mm needles cast on 96 sts in green.
Knit 2 rows.
Stocking stitch 23 rows.
*Next row:* P2 tog across row (48 sts).

**Join skirt to body—***Belt first row:* Hold body with skirt at front in left hand. Using navy, knit together one st from each needle.
*2nd row:* Knit (navy).
*3rd and 4th rows:* Knit (red).
*5th and 6th rows:* Knit (navy).

**Jumper:** Change to yellow, stocking stitch 18 rows.
Complete following directions for *Boy* from *Shape Shoulders.*

**Collar:** Beg at centre, pick up 14 sts for left side front. Knit 6 rows. Cast off. Rep for right side.

**Arms:** Follow directions for *Boy's Arm* from * to **. Change to yellow after joining cuff to arm and complete as for Boy omitting stripe.

## To make up

Using matching yarn ends, sew cast on edge and side seam of foot, inside leg, cuff and trousers of each leg. Sew centre back seam from legs to 3 cm from neck. To form foot, stitch through top and bottom at centre, from tip to last shaping row on underside, leaving two extra rows on underside un-stitched. Fill each side of foot with scraps of black yarn. Fold head in half with right side inside and sew from cast off edge at end of nose to neck. Sew ends of first two rows of head (bouclé) together at front neck. Leave rem row ends and cast on edge of head open. With centres matching sew row ends of head to cast off row of body at neck inside collar. Fill legs, body and head with polyester fibre. Insert eyes and check placement. Remove filling and attach metal backs. Close back head and jumper, filling as necessary to keep neck firm. Sew edges of boy's collar together at back. Sew cast on edges of ears to head above eyes. Sew hand and arm seam. Turn to right side. Fold arm with seam at centre on underside. Stitch hand through centre from tip to bouclé. Sew cuff and arm seam. Turn to right side and fill hand with scraps of black yarn. Fill arm with polyester fibre. Sew arm to body at shoulder inserting more filling if necessary. Sew button motifs at chest.

# Rabbit Sock Dolls

DESIGNED BY AMY BAHRT

This Easter, try giving something different —
some cuddly, friendly Rabbit Sock Dolls. They
can be as colourful as you choose — use bright
socks, contrasting embroidery and any
patchwork scraps on hand, to make bow ties or
decorations, such as initials, on their bodies.

*Rabbit Sock Dolls*

For the price of a pair of tube socks
from your local supermarket, you can
make *two* cute 25 cm bunny dolls. Dig
into your scrap bag for pink felt (for ear
linings) and some yarn for a woolly tail.
Follow our sketches below to make the
bunny's body and head from a 25 cm
toe portion of the sock; cut ears from
the remainder. Fill firmly with any
washable stuffing and sew on a smiling
face and two bright eyes with bits of
embroidery thread.

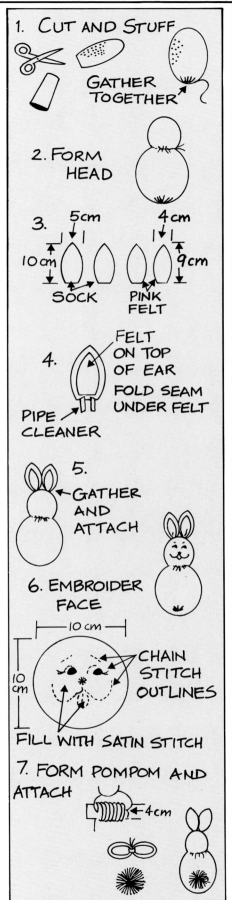

1. CUT AND STUFF
GATHER TOGETHER

2. FORM HEAD

3. 5cm 4cm
10cm 9cm
SOCK PINK FELT

4. FELT ON TOP OF EAR
FOLD SEAM UNDER FELT
PIPE CLEANER

5. GATHER AND ATTACH

6. EMBROIDER FACE
10 cm
10 cm
CHAIN STITCH OUTLINES
FILL WITH SATIN STITCH

7. FORM POMPOM AND ATTACH
4cm

# Mrs Roo & Little Kanga

DESIGNED BY SISTER MARY CHARITY

This makes an ideal gift for your family, or friends. An Australian pair to sew in fur fabric, or other soft, textured materials such as velvet, corduroy or suede. Mrs Roo is 53 cm tall; Kanga is 28 cm.

50 × 150 cm wide brown short pile fur fabric for both animals
40 × 70 cm wide piece white short pile fur fabric for both animals
one 25 mm black plastic nose
one 12 mm black plastic nose
two 20 mm brown/black glass eyes
two 15 mm brown/black glass eyes
sewing thread to match fabrics
polyester fibre filling
pencil, ruler, scissors
stiff paper for patterns
pins, needles, knitting needle, chalk
*Note:* Velvet, corduroy, suede-type fabrics can be substituted for fur fabric. Eyes and noses can be made from felt if preferred.

## TO MAKE TOYS

1. Following directions on pages 52–3, draw up patterns for mother and baby kangaroo, working to a scale of 1 sq = 2.5 cm. Before cutting out pattern pieces mark on all directions. *A 6 mm seam is allowed on all seams.*
2. Before placing pattern on fabric check the pile of fabric first. For fur fabrics have the smooth pile going down animal. For velvets have the rough going down. For other fabrics decide which you prefer.
3. Mark direction of pile on fabric with chalk and on pattern pieces. Place pattern on fabric and cut out.
4. Transfer lines indicating eye and nose placement to right side of fabric by basting with contrasting thread.
5. To assemble toys, pin pieces together with right sides facing and raw edges even; stitch easing in fullness where necessary; making 6 mm seams on all edges.

6. Clip into seam allowance at curves and across corners; turn to right side and poke out corners with knitting needle. Referring to photograph, assemble and finish each piece as directed below.

## MRS ROO

Read instructions above. Mark and cut the following from brown fur fabric: two head sides, one head centre, two ear backs, two body sides, two hips, and two pouch sides. From white fur fabric, cut two ear fronts, two body fronts, two soles. With contrasting thread, baste eye and nose fine lines as marked on pattern.

### To make ears
Stitch pair of ear fronts and backs together, leaving bases open; turn to right side. Turn raw edge 6 mm to inside and slipstitch openings closed.

### To make head
Stitch head sides to head centre matching A's and B's. Stitch head sides together matching A's and C's. Turn raw neck edge 6 mm to inside. Baste folded edge down. For glass eyes, make hole where indicated. Insert eyes from outside. Clamp on washers from inside. Repeat procedure with nose. Turn to right side. Stuff head with fibrefill until firm. Pin on ear, centred across each head side/centre seam; slip-stitch in place.

### To make body
Stitch pouch sides together matching G's and F's. Neaten raw edge and turn under 2.5 cm to inside. Baste folded edge down. Stitch body fronts together matching C's and F's. Baste pouch to body front matching E's and F's. Turn raw edge of body front neck edge, 6 mm to inside. Baste folded edge down. Stitch hip to body front matching E's and F's. Make dart in body sides. Turn

raw neck edge 6 mm to inside. Baste folded edge down. Stitch body sides to body front matching D's and E's and H's. Stitch body sides to body front matching F's and I's. Stitch body sides together matching F's and B's. Stitch soles to feet matching I's and H's. Slip-stitch head over neck, matching C's and B's, or turning it slightly.

## KANGA

Read instructions above first. Mark and cut the following from brown fur fabric: two head sides, one head centre, two ear backs, two body sides. From white fur fabric, cut two body fronts and two ear fronts. With contrasting thread, baste eye and nose fine lines as marked.

### To make ears
Follow directions for Mrs Roo.

### To make head
Follow directions for Mrs Roo.

### To make body
Stitch body fronts together matching C's and D's. Turn raw neck edge 6 mm inside. Baste folded edge down. Turn raw neck edge of body sides 6 mm inside. Baste folded edge down. Stitch body sides to body front matching E's and D's. Stitch body sides together matching D's and B's. Slipstitch head over neck matching C's and B's.

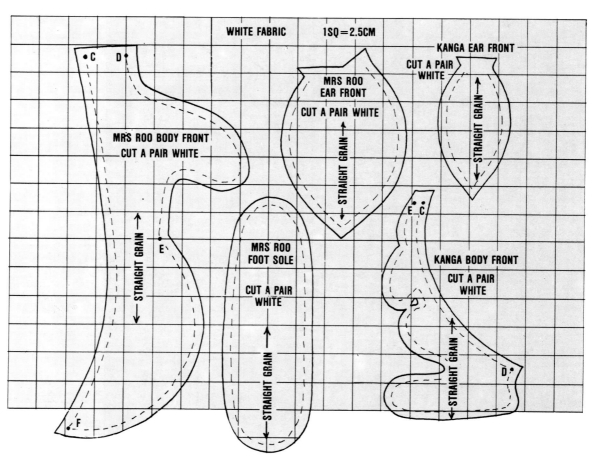

WHITE FABRIC    1SQ = 2.5CM

• C    D •

MRS ROO BODY FRONT
CUT A PAIR WHITE

STRAIGHT GRAIN

E •

F •

MRS ROO
EAR FRONT

CUT A PAIR WHITE

STRAIGHT GRAIN

KANGA EAR FRONT

CUT A PAIR
WHITE

STRAIGHT GRAIN

MRS ROO
FOOT SOLE

CUT A PAIR
WHITE

STRAIGHT GRAIN

E • • C

KANGA BODY FRONT

CUT A PAIR
WHITE

STRAIGHT GRAIN

D •

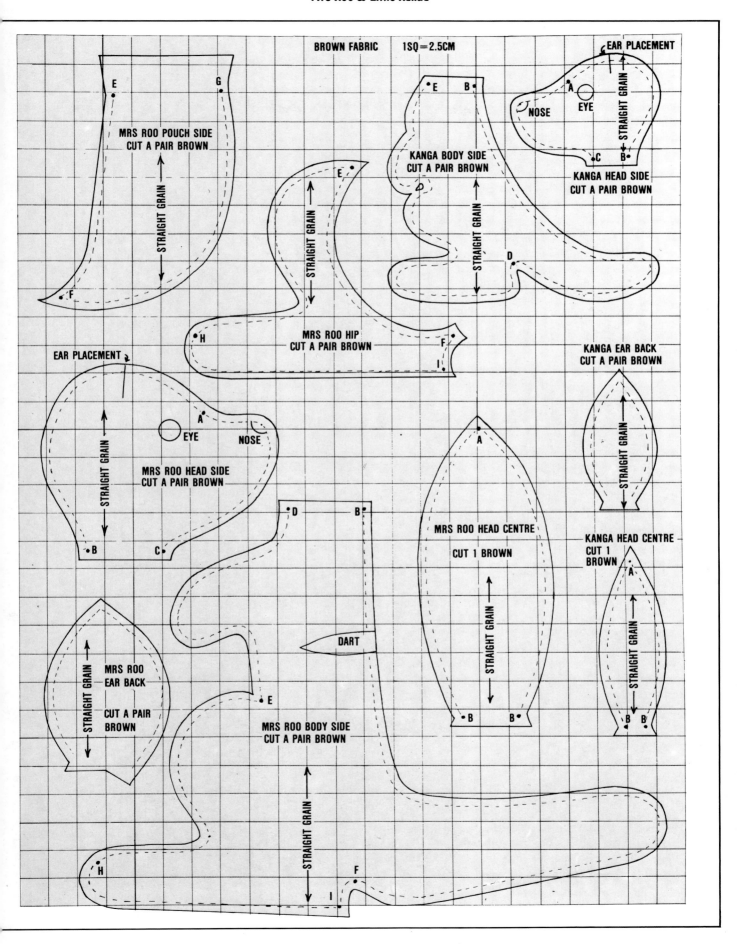

BROWN FABRIC    1SQ = 2.5CM

MRS ROO POUCH SIDE
CUT A PAIR BROWN

STRAIGHT GRAIN

E    G

F

KANGA BODY SIDE
CUT A PAIR BROWN

E    B

STRAIGHT GRAIN

D

EAR PLACEMENT

KANGA HEAD SIDE
CUT A PAIR BROWN

A

NOSE    EYE

C    B

STRAIGHT GRAIN

E

MRS ROO HIP
CUT A PAIR BROWN

H

F

I

KANGA EAR BACK
CUT A PAIR BROWN

STRAIGHT GRAIN

EAR PLACEMENT

MRS ROO HEAD SIDE
CUT A PAIR BROWN

STRAIGHT GRAIN

A

EYE    NOSE

B    C

D    B

MRS ROO HEAD CENTRE

CUT 1 BROWN

A

STRAIGHT GRAIN

B    B

KANGA HEAD CENTRE
CUT 1
BROWN

A

STRAIGHT GRAIN

B    B

MRS ROO
EAR BACK

CUT A PAIR
BROWN

STRAIGHT GRAIN

E

DART

MRS ROO BODY SIDE
CUT A PAIR BROWN

STRAIGHT GRAIN

H

F

I

*Crochet a Family of Hedgehogs*

# Crochet a Family of Hedgehogs

DESIGNED BY GWEN MERRILL

A lovable family of loopy hedgehogs.

Sirdar Pullman 12-ply (50 g balls)—
Baby 1 ball, Mum 2 balls, Dad 3 balls
1 pr 10 mm (Baby), 12 mm (Mum and Dad) plastic animal eyes
one 15 mm (Baby), two 18 mm (Mum and Dad) round buttons for nose
5.00 mm (No. 6) crochet hook
polyester fibrefilling
Baby 9 cm, Mum 12 cm, Dad 15 cm
*Tension:* 4 sts to 3.5 cm in width over loop stitch; 4 sts to 3 cm in width over double crochet.

Body is worked in rounds of double crochet and loop stitch beginning at the nose. There are no seams. The eyes are attached and body filled before completing final rounds.
*Loop stitch:* See p. 7. Loops are formed on back of work. For Baby hold finger close to work when forming loops, for Mum and Dad extend finger to make larger loops. Pull out loops to full length every 2 or 3 rounds. Loops can be cut if desired as stitch is locked.
*Abbreviations:* Alt — *alternate*; beg — *beginning*; ch — *chain*; dc — *double crochet*; dec — *decrease*; inc — *increase*; lp st — *loop stitch*; rnd(s) — *round(s)*; sl st — *slip stitch*; st — *stitch.*

## BABY

**Face:** Ch 2, 4 dc in first ch.
*2nd rnd:* Inc in every other dc (6 dc).
*3rd rnd:* Work 1 rnd.
*4th rnd:* Inc in every other dc (9 dc).
*5th rnd:* Inc in every 3rd dc (12 dc).
*6th rnd:* Inc in every other dc (18 dc).
*7th rnd:* Work 1 rnd.
**Body:** *8th rnd:* 1 dc, 17 lp sts.
*9th rnd:* 2 dc, 16 lp sts.
*10th rnd:* 3 dc, work 15 lp sts—inc in 3rd, 6th, 9th and 12th sts (22 sts).
*11th rnd:* 4 dc, 18 lp sts.
*12th rnd:* Rep 11th rnd.
*13th rnd:* 5 dc, work 17 lp sts—inc in 3rd, 7th, 11th and 15th sts (26 sts).
*14th rnd:* 5 dc, 21 lp sts.
*15th rnd:* 6 dc, 20 lp sts.
*16th rnd:* 6 dc, work 20 lp sts—inc in 3rd, 6th, 9th, 12th, 15th and 18th sts (32 sts).

*17th rnd:* 7 dc, 25 lp sts.
*18th rnd:* Rep 17th rnd.
*19th rnd:* 7 dc, 26 lp sts. *Note:* There is no increase in number of sts, extra lp st is worked for underbody shaping.
*20th rnd:* 6 dc, 27 lp sts.
*21st rnd:* 2 dc, miss 1 dc, 2 dc, work 22 lp sts—miss 4th, 9th, 14th, 19th and 24th sts (26 sts).
Continue in rnds of lp st, missing every 3rd st until 20 sts rem. Position eyes on face opposite underbody, attach backs. Fill face firmly with small pieces fibrefilling. Fill body softly. Continue to decrease every other stitch until opening is closed. Fasten off. Sew on button nose.

## MUM

**Face:** Ch 2, 4 dc in first ch.
*2nd rnd:* Inc in every other dc (6 dc).
*3rd rnd:* Work 1 rnd.
*4th rnd:* Inc in every other dc (9 dc).
*5th rnd:* Work 1 rnd.
*6th rnd:* Inc in every 3rd dc (12 dc).
*7th rnd:* Inc in every 3rd dc (16 dc).
*8th rnd:* Inc in every other dc (24 dc).
*9th rnd:* Work 1 rnd.
**Body:** *10th rnd:* 2 dc, 22 lp sts.
*11th rnd:* 3 dc, 21 lp sts.
*12th rnd:* 3 dc, work 21 lp sts—inc in 5th, 9th, 13th and 17th sts (28 sts).
*13th rnd:* 4 dc, 24 lp sts.
*14th rnd:* Rep 13th rnd.
*15th rnd:* 5 dc, 23 lp sts.
*16th rnd:* 5 dc, work 23 lp sts—inc in 3rd, 6th, 9th, 12th, 15th, 18th and 21st sts (35 sts).
*17th rnd:* 6 dc, 29 lp sts.
*18th rnd:* Rep 17th rnd.
*19th rnd:* 7 dc, 28 lp sts.
*20th rnd:* 7 dc, work 28 lp sts—inc in 4th, 7th, 10th, 13th, 16th, 19th, 22nd and 25th sts (43 sts).
*21st rnd:* 8 dc, 35 lp sts.
*22nd rnd:* Rep 21st rnd.
*23rd rnd:* 9 dc, 34 lp sts.
*24th rnd:* Rep 23rd rnd.
*25th rnd:* 9 dc, 35 lp sts. *Note:* There is no increase in number of stitches, extra lp st is worked for underbody shaping.
*26th rnd:* 8 dc, 36 lp sts.

*27th rnd:* 3 dc, miss 1 dc, 3 dc—work 30 lp sts miss 6th, 11th, 16th, 21st, 26th and 31st sts (36 sts). Continue in rnds of lp st dec every 4th stitch until 20 sts rem. Position eyes on face opposite underbody, attach backs. Fill face firmly with small pieces of fibrefilling. Fill body softly. Continue to decrease every 3rd st until 8 sts rem, then every other st until opening is closed. Fasten off. Sew button on nose.

## DAD

**Face:** Ch 2, 6 dc in first ch.
*2nd rnd:* Inc in every other dc (9 dc).
*3rd rnd:* Work 1 rnd.
*4th rnd:* Inc in every 3rd dc (12 dc).
*5th rnd:* Work 1 rnd.
*6th rnd:* Inc in every 3rd dc (16 dc).
*7th rnd:* Inc in every other dc (24 dc).
*8th rnd:* Inc in every 6th dc (28 dc).
*9th and 10th rnds:* Work even in dc.
**Body:** *11th rnd:* 2 dc, 26 lp sts.
*12th rnd:* Rep 11th rnd.
*13th rnd:* 3 dc, work 25 lp sts—inc in 3rd, 7th, 11th, 15th, 19th and 23rd sts (34 sts).
*14th rnd:* 3 dc, 31 lp sts.
*15th rnd:* 4 dc, 30 lp sts.
*16th rnd:* Rep 15th rnd.
*17th rnd:* 5 dc, 29 lp sts.
*18th rnd:* 5 dc, work 29 lp sts—inc in 3rd, 7th, 11th, 15th, 19th, 23rd and 27th sts (41 sts).
*19th rnd:* 6 dc, 35 lp sts.
*20th rnd:* Rep 19th rnd.
*21st rnd:* 7 dc, 34 lp sts.
*22nd rnd:* Rep 21st rnd.
*23rd rnd:* 8 dc, work 33 lp sts—inc in 3rd, 7th, 11th, 15th, 19th, 23rd, 27th and 31st sts (49 sts).
*24th rnd:* 8 dc, 41 lp sts.
*25th rnd:* 9 dc, 40 lp sts.
*26th rnd:* Rep 25th rnd.
*27th rnd:* 10 dc, 39 lp sts.
*28th rnd:* 10 dc, 40 lp sts. *Note:* There is no increase in number of stitches, extra lp st is worked for underbody shaping.
*29th rnd:* 9 dc, 41 lp sts.
*30th rnd:* 8 dc, 42 lp sts.
*31st rnd:* 3 dc, miss 1 dc, 3 dc, work 36 lp sts—dec 6th, 12th, 18th, 24th, 30th and 36th sts (42 sts).
Continue in rnds of lp st dec every 5th stitch until 20 sts rem. Position eyes on face opposite underbody, attach backs. Fill face firmly with small pieces of fibre. Fill body softly. Continue to dec every 4th st until 8 sts rem, then every other st until opening is closed. Fasten off. Sew button on to hedgehog's nose.

# Playmice to Knit

DESIGNED BY GWEN MERRILL

Knit these friendly mice with their striped jumpers and colourful overalls. Mr Mouse stands 36 cm high; Squeaky 27 cm.

The mice are knitted in 8-ply yarn on finer needles than usual to give a firmer texture.

*Squeaky*
One yellow and two navy 25 g balls of yarn
small quantities light brown, red, blue, green, purple yarn
two 10 mm buttons

*Mr Mouse*
Two each navy and green, one each light brown, white and red 25 g balls yarn
two 15 mm buttons

*Both mice*
Polyester fibre filling
1 pr 3 mm (No. 11) knitting needles
tapestry needle for sewing seams

*Abbreviations:* K — *knit*; P — *purl*; st(s) — *stitch(es)*; cont — *continue*; tog — *together*; st st — *stocking stitch*; inc — *increase*; dec — *decrease*; rep — *repeat*; alt — *alternate*; foll — *following*; beg — *beginning*; patt — *pattern*; psso — *pass slip stitch over*; M1 — *make 1*.

*Note:* Instructions for Mr Mouse are given in brackets. Where one set of figures or instructions is given this applies to both sizes.

## Back body

Cast on 15 (21) sts in yellow (*green*) for overall.

*1st row:* Knit.
*2nd row:* Knit. Inc at each end of row.
Rep these 2 rows until 29 (43) sts*. Knit 16 (22) rows. Join in navy, knit 4 rows. Join in red (*white*) st st 4 rows. Join in blue (*red*) st st 4 rows. *Mr Mouse only:* St st 2 rows white, keeping stripe and colour pattern correct (*see photograph*).
Dec first and last st in next and foll knit rows until 21 (25) sts rem. Work 6 (7) rows without shaping.
*Shape armhole:* Dec first and last st in

next 3 knit rows—15 (19) sts. Cast off 1 (3) sts at beg of the next 2 rows—13 sts.

## Roll neck collar

K12 rows green (*red*), cast off loosely.

## Head

Using light brown knit up 13 sts on wrong side, from first row of collar.
*2nd and alt rows:* Purl.
*3rd row:* Inc first and last st in next and foll K rows until 23 (25) sts. Work 3 (5) rows without shaping. Dec first and last st in next and foll knit rows until 13 sts remain. Cast off.

## Front body

Work as for back to 29 (43) sts*. Knit 15 (21) rows.
*Next row:* K21 (31) turn.
*Next row:* K13 (19) turn.

## Bib

K10 (14) rows on these 13 (19) sts. *Mr Mouse only:* K14 rows, dec first and last st in next and foll 8th row (15 sts).
*Next row (both sizes):* Make buttonholes 2 sts from ends of row. Cast off 1 (2) sts in this row. Cast on 1 (2) sts in foll row. Knit one row.
*Next row:* Join in navy, inc first and last st of next 2 rows. Cast off. With wrong side of work facing, knit up 13 (19) sts at back of bib in yellow (*green*) and knit remaining 8 (12) sts on left-hand needle. Join in navy.
*1st row:* Knit.
*2nd row:* K8 (12), P13 (19), K8 (12). Rep these 2 rows once. Join in red (*white*) and foll patt for back.
*To complete bib:* Working from right side pick up 11 (16) sts along side of bib. Knit 2 rows, inc once at top of bib. Cast off. Rep for other side.

## Arms

With right sides together sew front and back together around head and from neck to top of armhole (*straight section*).

With right side facing knit up 16 (18) sts in red across back and front armhole. St st 5 (9) rows keeping stripe correct. Dec first and last st in next row—14 (16) sts.
*Mr Mouse only:* St st 7 rows. Dec first and last st in 4th row (14 sts).

## Cuff (both sizes)

K6 rows in red. Join in light brown, st st 7 rows dec first and last st in 3rd row. Cast off. Rep for other arm.

## Ears

*Outer ear (work two):* Cast on 20 sts in navy.
*1st row:* Purl.
*Slip first st, K4, M1, K to last 5 sts, M1, K5 (22 sts).*
*3rd and foll purl rows:* Slip first st knitways, P to last st, K1.
Rep 2nd and 3rd rows until 30 (32) sts. Work 2 (4) rows without shaping continuing to slip first st.
Slip 1, K3, slip 1, K1, psso, K to last 6 sts, K2 tog, K4—28 (30) sts.
*Next row:* Slip first st knitways, P to last st, K1. Rep last 2 rows until 18 sts remain.
*Next row:* K2 tog, K2, slip 1, K1, psso, K2 tog 4 times, K2, K2 tog (11 sts).
*Next row:* Purl.
*Next row:* Slip 1, K2, slip 1, K1, psso, K1, K2 tog, K3 (9 sts).
*Next row:* Purl.
*Next row:* K2 tog, K1, K3 tog, K1, K2 tog (5 sts). Cast off.
*Inner ear (work two):* Cast on 6 sts in light brown.
*1st row:* Purl.
*2nd row:* Inc, K to last st inc. Rep these two rows until 16 (20) sts.
Work 1 (3) rows without shaping.
*Next row:* Dec, K to last 2 sts dec.
*Next row:* Purl. Rep these two rows until 6 sts remain. Cast off.

## Feet (work four)

Cast on 15 (19) sts in navy. Beg with a purl row st st 13 (17) rows. Dec first and last st of next and foll K rows until 5 sts rem. Cast off.

## Tail

Cast on 8 (9) sts in navy. St st until work measures 30 (36) cm. Dec first and last st of next and foll K rows until 2 (3) sts rem. Cast off.

## To make up

With right sides facing continue sewing body sections together using a machine for a neater finish. Leave body open at base. Sew in ends of yarn securely. Turn to right side and join seams of roll neck collar. Fill head and neck firmly. Body and arms require less filling. Close body opening. Sew inner to outer ear with right sides facing, matching corresponding shaping rows. Leave open at base. Turn to right side and fill. Position ears on sides of head and secure with matching yarns. Join navy trim on bib front at corners.

*To make braces:* Knit up 4 sts in navy 3 (5) cm from side seams at the back. Knit 15 (20). cm and cast off. Mark position of buttons and sew to right side of braces.

*Feet:* Sew feet with right sides facing. Leave open at straight end. Turn to right side, fill and stitch across opening. Sew feet to body along base seam. Bring foot forward by stitching top of foot to body at the front.

*Tail:* Roll sides of tail together and sew row ends from right side. Sew tail to body between legs.

*Face:* Embroider face in navy.

**FACES**

# Cuddly Sock Toys

### A treasure chest of garden creatures.

These toys can be made from socks or closely woven knitted fabrics such as velvet or towelling stretch fabrics, discarded sweaters or knit pants. You can also use brightly coloured striped and plain socks. The feet or top of pastel bed socks or fleecy lined infants' clothing can be used to make the chicken, rabbit or frog. Stuff with polyester fibre filling and decorate.

1. If the sock dosen't fill well because it is too thin or stretchy, fill an old nylon stocking first and pull the sock over it.

2. The width or length of a toy will depend on the stretch of sock or fabric

*Cuddly Sock Toys*

used. Measurements given are only approximate and may need adjusting.

**To make a tube**

Cut stretch fabric approximately 24 cm by required length. Fold in half length-wise with right side inside. Pin and machine zigzag down side 1 cm in from raw edge. Trim to stitching and zigzag stitch again.

2. With double thread put a row of running stitches around one end. Pull up to approximately 5 cm and machine across twice to hold. Turn through to right side and stuff. Following directions given for individual toys, finish the top the same as the bottom if required.

3. Stitch over each end by hand to remove puckers and give a well-rounded look to bottom and top.

## GREEN STRIPED CATERPILLAR

1. Use a striped tube sock or prepared tube (*see above*), approximately 30 cm long. Stuff it up to 5 cm from opening. Tie securely closed above stuffing and pull top of sock down over head. If sock does not have a white top follow directions for Eggplant, Step 4.

2. To form four legs on one side, starting at the toe seam, make four 4 cm circles with small running stitches, pull up to form 2 cm knobs; knot thread securely.

3. Just below ribbed edge, sew on two 6 mm brown felt circles 2 cm apart for eyes; below eyes, sew on two 3.5 cm pink circles 2.5 cm apart.

## BLUSHING PEA

Cut 16.5 cm from toe of green ankle sock. Make running stitches around sock, 2.5 cm from cut edge. Turn in top to stitch line. Stuff with polyester fibre filling until firm. Pull up stitching and knot securely. Sew on two 6 mm black circles, 2 cm apart for eyes; below them sew on two 4 cm pink felt circles, 12 mm apart.

## YELLOW CHICK

1. Stuff foot of a pale yellow bed sock to ankle, with towelling or fluffy side on the outside. Cut off and whipstitch ankle edges together. Alternatively, make a tube cut approximately 24 × 24 cm (*see above*).

2. Approximately 4 cm from top of head, sew on two 6 mm circles of dark felt, 2 cm apart for eyes. Below eyes,

sew across centre of a 3.5 cm pink felt circle; fold down top half to form bill.

3. Tie a piece of ribbon around chick 7.5 cm from top of head, pulling in slightly to indicate neck.

## FROG

1. Stuff a women's size green sock to ankle. Whipstitch ankle edges together. Alternatively, make a tube cut approximately 24 × 24 cm wide (*see above*).

2. To form each eye bulge, make a circle approximately 10 cm deep from back to front of small running stitches around a top corner. Pull up thread to form rounded bulge and fasten thread end securely at the whipstitched seam.

3. *Eyes:* Sew a 2 cm lavender circle at centre of 3.5 cm yellow circle to make an eye. With ankle seam at the back, sew an eye to centre of each bulge, touching the running stitch. Cut a 4 cm green circle in half, sew one half over top part of each eye.

4. Tack down a scrap of orange yarn for mouth.

## RABBIT

1. Use a women's size bed sock with towelling or fluffy side outside. Alternatively, make a tube cut approximately 26 × 24 cm wide.

2. *To make ears from sock:* Measure and mark a centre line, 6 cm down from edge of toe. Draw in ears, 6 mm each side of centre line. Stitch on drawn lines. Slash on centre line. Turn right side out.

*To make ears from tube:* Fold seam to centre back, mark down 6.5 cm from top and stitch as above. Put a row of gathering around each end of ear, pull up firmly. Turn ear to right side. Ear can be stuffed lightly to make it stand up if fabric is too soft.

3. Make small running stitches across bottom of ears, curving down at outside. Stuff below ears. Cut sock off at ankle and whipstitch edges together.

4. Measure 5 cm down from top of head, sew on two 6 mm blue felt circles 2.5 cm apart for eyes. Tie a ribbon into a bow 7.5 cm down from top of head, pulling in slightly to indicate the neck.

## RED/BLACK BEETLE

1. Use a striped tube sock or prepared tube (*see above*), approximately 30 cm long. Stuff it up to 10 cm from opening.

2. Make running stitches around end just above stuffing, tuck in end, pull up

stitches and knot securely to form mouth. Flatten body slightly.

3. At each side of body, start at toe seam and make three 4 cm circles with small running stitches; pull up thread to form 2 cm knobs.

4. Knot securely. Sew a 2 cm green felt circle at edge of a 3.5 cm white circle. Repeat to make two eyes. Sew eyes 2.5 cm from mouth and 6 mm apart.

## BLACK/WHITE STRIPED WORM

Use a black and white striped tube sock or prepared tube (*see above*), approximately 58 cm long. Stuff up to 25 cm from the toe and tie remaining sock in a large knot just above the stuffing. Approximately 7.5 cm down from the knot, sew on two 1 cm lavender circles, 12 mm apart for eyes; below eyes sew on two 3.5 cm pink felt circles, about 12 mm apart. To form hat, cut 21.5 cm off the top of an old ribbed sock. Gather up the cut edge and tie securely, 12 mm down from the edge. Turn right side out. Stuff top of hat with a ball of fibrefill. Pull hat over the sock knot and roll up hat edges.

## EGGPLANTS

*Note:* Numbers in brackets are for the large eggplant.

1. Turn a purple ankle sock to the inside approximately 20 cm (25 cm) from the top and stuff.

2. Make running stitches around folded edge and pull them up, leaving a small opening. Knot thread securely.

3. Approximately 7.5 cm (10 cm) down from the top, sew on two 1 cm light blue or black circles for eyes, 2 cm apart.

4. For hat, stuff the foot section of a child's ankle sock into the eggplant opening, letting 7.5 cm (10 cm) extend. Turn over green cuff and sew edges in place 12 mm above the eyes.

# Lucy & her Bear

A gorgeous blond in a sailor suit accompanied by her teddy bear. You can make her a brunette or a redhead, by using different coloured fur fabric or wool. Lucy is 39 cm tall, her bear 15 cm.

30 × 115 cm wide flesh-tone fabric for doll
20 × 23 cm piece light gold long-haired fur fabric for doll's hair
50 × 115 cm wide white fabric
30 × 115 cm wide blue fabric
50 cm of 6 mm elastic
four press-studs
1.8 m narrow white braid
23 × 30 cm piece black felt
two pearl buttons (optional)
60 cm each 12 mm wide and 5 cm wide red ribbon
23 × 50 cm wide piece brown fur fabric or other short pile fabric for bear
12 mm piece Velcro tape fastener
polyester fibrefill
fabric crayons, paint or pastels for face
red and black embroidery thread for dress trim and bear face

*Note:* Offcuts of long-haired nylon fur fabric are sometimes available from bargain fabric stores. A scrap of dyed lambswool could be substituted for wig or strands of thick wool could be teased out and stitched to the head.

Following directions on page 6, enlarge patterns in Figs. 1-3. Be sure to label patterns including 'Fold', where indicated. These pieces must be cut from double fabric with the pattern edge marked 'Fold' matching the fabric fold. See page 62 for patterns.

Cut out patterns (*see directions for face, below*). Patterns include 5 mm seams. Pin, stitch seam edges with right sides facing.

## LUCY

1. *Cut doll, flesh-tone fabric:* Cut centre head, one pair of side heads, body front, body back, two pairs of arms, two legs, two upper feet, and two foot soles. *Fur fabric:* Cut wig centre and a pair of wig sides.

*Lucy & Her Bear*

*Note:* To cut a pair, cut one piece with pattern right side up and one with pattern right side down.

2. *Face:* With fabric crayons, paint or pastels, colour features on face as follows: Eyes—blue; upper lip and lip line—bright pink; lower lip and nose—pink; highlight at tip of nose—white; cheeks—pale pink, slightly darker than fabric; nostrils—red. Following manufacturer's directions, iron colours onto fabric.

3. *Head:* Seam side heads to centre head, leave bottom edges open. Turn to right side and stuff firmly, filling out curves and rounding cheeks.

4. *Arms:* Leaving top edges open, seam two arms; turn. Stuff lower half firmly, upper half lightly; leave last few centimetres unstuffed. With seamlines matching, turn in seam allowances at top and slipstitch closed. Repeat for other arm.

5. *Legs:* Seam upper foot to leg at ankle edges; then stitch centre back seam from top to bottom, leaving upper edges open. Stitch sole to foot matching centres. Turn and stuff firmly. With seam centred, turn in opening edges and slipstitch closed.

6. *Body:* Seam dart edges on body back; clip darts at side seams. Leaving neck edges open, seam body back to body front. Turn and stuff firmly, filling out curves and corners.

7. *Assemble doll:* Pin head to body with head overlapping and centres matching; slipstitch. Thumbs facing up, pin and slipstitch arm to body 6 mm from neck seam. Pin and slipstitch legs to lower body seam, matching side edges.

8. *Hair:* Seam wig side pieces to wig centre, smoothing strands away from seams. Clip to seamlines at curves. Matching seams, place wig on doll's head and slipstitch in place by hand. Brush hair down from centre and trim off ends approximately 2.5 cm all around wig.

## LUCY'S CLOTHING

1. *Cut clothing, white fabric:* Cut middy, waistband, two jumpers, trim on dotted line for front neckline, two sleeves and two bloomers. *Blue fabric:* Cut skirt front, skirt back, collar, collar facing and two cuffs. *Black felt:* Cut two shoe uppers and two shoe soles.

2. With red embroidery thread, using straight stitches, embroider anchor on jumper front, 2 cm from neck edge and stripes on centre of left sleeve (*see Fig. 2A*). Stitch braid approximately 1 cm from side edges of collar and trim ends flush with collar edges. Stitch braid to back edge of collar the same way. Stitch second row of braid a little inside the first.

3. *Middy:* Easing in fullness, seam head of sleeve to armholes. Fold cuffs in half lengthwise, right sides in, gather bottom of sleeve to fit cuff and seam folded cuff to sleeve edge. Stitch braid on cuff to match collar trim. Then stitch entire cuff, sleeve and side seam at each side. Clip underarms and turn right side out. Seam facing to collar; turn to right side and baste raw edges together. Pin right side of collar to *wrong* side of middy neck edge matching centres and x's; stitch seam and clip curves. At centre front edges of middy turn under 12 mm and topstitch.

Fold waistband in half lengthwise right side out; turn under ends 12 mm.

Gather lower edge of middy to fit waistband; pin and stitch folded waistband to middy edge right sides together. Press waistband downward. Sew press-studs to front opening at neck and waistband. Knot a 23 cm length of 6 mm ribbon in the centre and sew it onto the front of middy, below collar.

4. *Jumper:* On skirt front and back mark dots and dashes for pleats. Stitch side seams and stitch a 2 cm hem at lower edge. To form pleats, fold at dots and bring each fold to nearest dash; press pleats.

On jumper front and back, make a narrow hem by hand around neck and armholes. Seam front and back together at sides only. Turn under ends of shoulder straps 6 mm and sew on press-studs. At lower edge, turn up 6 mm and press. Matching side seams, pin turned edge of jumper over upper edge of pleated skirt. Topstitch.

5. *Bloomers:* To form casings, turn waist and leg edges under 3 mm and then 1

**FIG 1 DOLL BODY**

1SQ = 2.5cm

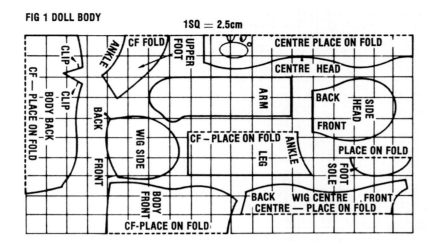

each long straight edge of head gusset to one front, from top of head to nose, clipping front seam at nose corners.

3. Pin back pieces together along centre back seam; starting at top of head, stitch for 5 cm. Then, starting at crotch, stitch for 4 cm, leaving centre of seam open for styling.

4. Stitch ears together, except at straight edge and turn right side out. With raw edges matching and right sides together, baste ears to front with each ear starting at a gusset seam.

5. Pin and seam front to back all around. Clip at crotch, underarms and neck and turn right side out. Stuff, filling out curves of head, arms and legs. Slipstitch opening closed. Where arms and legs join body, sew running stitch through all thicknesses to create joints.

6. With black embroidery thread and straight stitches, embroider eyes and nose. Tie narrow ribbon bow around neck. Sew remaining piece of tape fastener to back of right paw and attach Teddy to Lucy's hand.

cm; stitch. Insert 10 cm length of elastic at each waist and 11.5 cm length at each leg. Stitch the two pieces together at centre front and centre back seams, catching in ends of elastic. Stitch two crotch seams to form legs. Turn right side out.

6. *Shoes:* With red thread, topstitch around upper edges and cutouts. Stitch back seams, using black thread. Pin and seam uppers to soles matching centres, turn right side out. If desired, sew button to each shoe as shown in photograph.

7. *Dress Lucy:* Sew simple tubes closed at one end from finely woven black ankle socks.

Put stockings on first, then bloomers. To put on shoes, first slip them over toes; then compress heels and slip on shoes. Put on jumper and middy; arrange bloomer legs just above skirt hem. Tie wide ribbon bow; sew or pin to hair as shown. Cut tape fastener into two 6 mm pieces. Sew one to left hand 6 mm from fingertips. Brush hair, teasing ends slightly upward.

## TEDDY BEAR

1. *Cut Bear, fur fabric:* Cut gusset, pair of fronts, pair of backs and four ears, two of these are ear facings. Have the nap going downward.

*Note:* To cut a pair, cut one piece with pattern right side up and one with pattern right side down.

2. Pin and stitch front pieces together along centre front seam from crotch to nose. Pin centre front seam to gusset, right sides together, matching seam to centre of short straight, nose edge of gusset. Stitch across the nose edge. Pin

**FIG 2 LUCY DOLL CLOTHES**

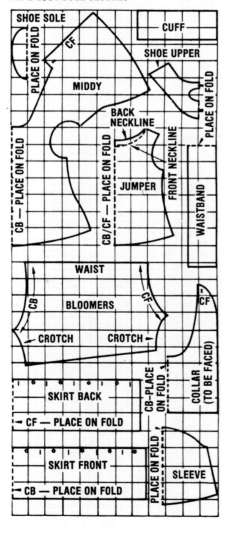

**FIG 3 TEDDY BEAR**

1SQ = 2.5cm

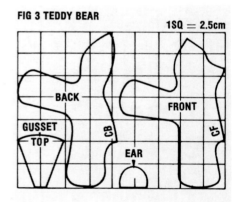

**FIG 2A EMBROIDERY (LUCY DOLL CLOTHES) ACTUAL SIZE PATTERNS**

# Three Lions to Crochet

DESIGNED BY GWEN MERRILL

Woolly lions in bright colours stand about 23 cm high.

*Three Lions to Crochet*

Small quantities Patons Totem 8-ply yarn
scraps of black felt for eyes
black yarn for nose and mouth
3.50 mm (No. 9) crochet hook
1 pair 9 mm plastic animal safety eyes
tapestry needle
polyester fibre for filling
The body and legs are worked in rnds of double crochet starting at the neck. The head is worked in rnds of double crochet then loop stitch commencing at the nose. The eyes and filling are inserted before completing final rnds at back of head. Do not join rnds unless specified. Work in a spiral fashion using a safety pin or yarn to mark the beg of each rnd. Always change colour on last st of rnd, drawing loop of new colour through last 2 loops on hook.
*Note:* The colours specified in the pattern can be changed to suit.
*Abbreviations:* Alt — *alternate;* beg — *beginning;* ch — *chain;* dc — *double crochet;* dec — *decrease;* inc — *increase;* lp st — *loop stitch (see directions on page 50);* rnd(s) — *round(s);* sl st — *slip stitch;* st — *stitch.*

## Head

*(Modelled on yellow lion)*
Starting at centre of nose with yellow, ch 2.
*1st rnd:* 6 dc in 2nd ch from hook, sl st to join rnd.
*2nd rnd:* 1 dc in each dc around.
*3rd rnd:* Inc in every other dc around (9 dc).
*4th rnd:* 1 dc in each dc around.
*5th rnd:* Inc in every dc around (18 dc). Tie marker on last dc.
*6th rnd:* 9 dc, tie marker; *forehead shaping*—2 dc, inc in next dc, 3 dc, inc in next dc, 2 dc (20 dc).
*7th rnd:* 12 dc, in next dc, 3 dc, inc in next dc, 3 dc, (22 dc).
*8th rnd:* 9 dc, 13 lp sts.
*9th rnd:* 8 dc, work 14 lp sts inc in 2nd, 5th, 8th, 11th, 14th sts (27 sts).
*10th rnd:* 3 lp sts, 3 dc, work 21 lp sts, inc in 5th, 10th, 15th, 20th sts (31 sts).
*11th rnd:* 4 lp sts, 2 dc, 25 lp sts.
*12th and 13th rnds:* 1 lp st in each st.
*14th rnd:* Dec every 3rd st around (21 sts).
Cut black felt shape for back of eyes, pierce hole at centre and insert plastic eyes and position on face on forehead section. Attach metal backs to eyes and then fill the head with polyester fibre. Continue in rnds of lp st, dec every 3rd st around until opening is closed. Fasten off.

## Body

*Note:* For striped section alternate 2 rnds of each colour until 12th rnd. Change colour on last st of rnd drawing lp of new colour through last 2 lps on hook.
Starting at neck edge with white, ch 14. Join with a sl st to form ring.
*1st rnd:* Ch 1, dc in same ch as sl st 1 dc in each ch around (14 dc).
*2nd and alt rnds:* 1 dc in each dc around.
*3rd rnd:* Inc 1 dc in every other dc around (21 dc).
*5th rnd:* Inc 3 dc evenly around (24 dc).
*7th rnd:* Inc 4 dc evenly around (28 dc).
*9th rnd:* Inc 4 dc evenly around (32 dc).
*10th, 11th and 12th rnds:* 1 dc in each dc around.
Change colour for lower body.
*13th and 14th rnds:* 1 dc in each dc around.
*15th rnd:* Dec 4 dc evenly around (28 dc).
*16th rnd:* 1 dc in each dc around.
*17th rnd:* Dec 4 dc evenly around (24 dc).
*18th and 19th rnds:* Dec 2 dc evenly around (20 dc).

Sl st in next st.
*1st leg opening:* Ch 3, miss next 9 dc, sl st in next dc for 1st leg opening; ch 1, do not turn.
*1st leg:* *1st rnd:* 1 dc in each of next 9 dc, 1 dc in each of 3 ch (12 dc). Work 8 rnds without shaping.
*10th rnd—shaping for front foot:* (1 dc in next dc, inc in next dc) twice, 1 dc to end of rnd (14 dc).
*11th rnd:* Inc 2 dc above those in last rnd, dc to end of rnd (16 dc).
*12th rnd:* 1 dc in each dc around.
*13th rnd—base of foot:* Work 1 dc into inside lp only of every other dc of previous rnd (8 dc).
*14th rnd:* (1 dc in every other dc) 3 times, miss 1, sl 1, break off*.
*2nd leg:* Join in yarn at leg opening and work from * to * of 1st leg, working foot shaping in *reverse.*

## Arms

*(Make two)*
With red, ch 2.
*1st rnd:* Work 8 dc in 2nd ch from hook. Work even for 6 rnds, break off red. Fill arm, flatten out. Using yellow work through both thicknesses for hand as follows:
*1st row:* 4 dc, 1 ch, turn. *2nd row:* 4 dc, turn. *3rd row:* Miss first dc, 3 dc. Work 2 sl sts back over row ends along side of hand.

**Thumb:** 3 ch, 1 dc in first ch, work sl st into side of hand, fasten off.
*Note:* For purple Lion body, work to 9th rnd in red then 10th, 11th and 12th rnds in dark purple.

## To make up

Sew in yarn ends. Fill legs and lower body through neck opening. Sew section without lp sts at base of head to neck inserting more filling if necessary. Sew arms to body at sides with thumbs upwards. Embroider nose and mouth in satin stitch with black yarn following photograph.

# Mr Bunny Rabbit

He's about 75 cm tall, and takes his own carrots wherever he goes!

1 dinner plate 27 cm diam, for pattern
1 side plate 16 cm diam, for pattern
90 cm white fake fur 150 cm wide
20 cm pink fake fur 150 cm wide
matching thread
invisible nylon thread
3 m black embroidery thread
120 cm (35 mm wide) gingham ribbon
approx 1.5 kg polyester fibrefill
fabric adhesive
small amount pink yarn
2 sheets brown paper each 80 × 55 cm
dressmaker's chalk
ruler

## To make pattern

**Body and face:** Trace dinner plate on one sheet of brown paper and label circle 'A'. Now, overlap the dinner plate on circle A so that the width across the middle of the two plates is 43 cm (see Fig. 1 page 66). Label this second circle 'B'. Trace a third circle 'C', overlapping A and B so that the height measures 46 cm. Trace side plate on brown paper just above circle C. Do not overlap. Label circle 'D'. For circle 'E', overlap the plate on circle D so that the width across the middle of these two plates measures 28 cm. Trace a third circle 'F' overlapping D and E so that the height measures 27 cm. Before cutting, fill out the sides of the body and face with dotted lines so you have a smooth flowing line for cutting (see diagram in Fig. 1). Label ear, arm and foot positions on pattern as indicated. Cut pattern following outside lines.

On second sheet of brown paper trace remaining pieces and cut out.

**Pouch:** Trace dinner plate and label circle '2A'. Overlap the dinner plate on circle 2A so that the width across the middle of the two plates is 43 cm. Label this second circle '2B'. Join the two circles with a line to form a smooth curve.

**Tail and nose:** Trace side plate on brown paper twice. Label one 'tail' and one 'nose'.

**Ears and feet:** Trace dinner plate on brown paper twice. Label one 'ears' and the other 'feet'.

**Inside of ear:** Draw a rectangle 6.5 × 27 cm. Round off both ends to form a curve. Label this 'inside of ear'.

**Arms:** Draw a rectangle 9 × 27 cm. Round off one end to form a smooth curve. Label this 'arms'.

## To cut out

Place pattern pieces on the wrong side of a single thickness of fabric. Start with the larger pieces and fit the smaller ones in around them. Place each pattern piece so the nap runs from top to bottom on each body piece. (To determine the direction of the nap, stroke the fabric. If it feels smooth, you are stroking with the nap.) Trace around each piece with chalk.

Cut out the following pieces, carefully trying to avoid cutting the nap on the right side by snipping through the back only with the point of the scissors:

| White fake fur: | Pink fake fur: |
|---|---|
| 1 pouch | 1 nose |
| 2 bodies | 1 tail |
| 2 feet | 2 inside ears |
| 2 ears | |
| 4 arms | |

## To make rabbit

*Note:* Use 12 mm seam allowance throughout.

**Arms:** Stitch 2 arm pieces together, right sides together, leaving open at top. Trim seam allowance. Clip curves. Turn right side out. Stuff carefully, filling the arm without any gaps. Pack the stuffing tightly. A firmly stuffed toy looks better and is more durable. Fill to within 2.5 cm of top. Close with a line of machine stitching.

**Feet:** Fold feet in half, with right sides together. Stitch leaving a 7.5 cm opening for stuffing. Trim seam allowances. Clip curves. Turn right side out. Stuff. Fill to within 2.5 cm of top. Close opening by hand.

**Ears:** Glue pink inside of ear to centre portion of main ear with wrong sides together. Roll outer edges of circle to middle (leaving enough pink showing for inside of ear). Hand sew the rolled portion in place. Bring tip of ear and base of ear to a point and overcast by hand.

**Pouch:** Turn under 5 cm on top edge of pouch. Hem with a line of machine stitching or hem by hand.

**Body:** Pin and baste ears in place on right side of body front, as marked by x's in diagram (see Fig. 1). Pin and baste arms in place on right side of body front, as marked by o's in diagram. Pin and baste pouch in place having wrong side of pouch and right side of body front together. Stitch body back to body front with right sides together. Catch ears and arms in seam line. Leave a 15 cm opening at base of rabbit. Trim seam allowances. Clip curves. Turn right side out. Stuff firmly, filling cheeks and shoulders carefully. Close bottom seam.

**Tail:** Run a gathering thread around the entire outer edge of tail piece. Pull up into a ball, stuffing firmly as you go. Place in position against body back, flattening the ball shape slightly. Apply a dab of fabric adhesive to the back of the tail before sewing. Attach by sewing securely around outer edge.

**Nose:** Follow the method for tail, placing nose in position on face.

**Face:** With black thread, embroider a smiling mouth using stem stitch. Embroider the eyes (approximately the size of five cents) using a satin stitch.

**Arms and feet:** With the black thread, embroider 4 fingers on tip of arms, each 13 mm apart and 2.5 cm long. Use stem stitch. To attach feet to body, use invisible nylon thread. Securely stitch centre of curved edge of feet to bottom of body (see diagram in Fig. 1). Also, attach heels of feet together with an overcast stitch.

To hang up rabbit, attach a loop of yarn to top of head. Tie ribbon around neck.

**Mr Bunny Rabbit — Fig 1**

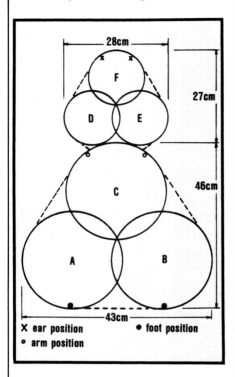

X ear position    ● foot position
○ arm position

# Dear Little Dolls to Knit

DESIGNED BY GWEN MERRILL

They're only about 12 cm high and would make perfect gifts for girls and boys of all ages.

Small quantities of 4, 5, or 6-ply wool in bright colours for bodies and faces bouclé wool for hair
1 pr 2.75 (No. 12) knitting needles
tapestry needle for sewing seams
2.00 (No. 7) crochet hook
polyester fibre for filling

Each doll is knitted in one piece. The arms and legs are formed by stitching through all layers after doll has been sewn up and filled. The neck and feet are pulled in with gathering threads. Thicker wool can be used for hair, belt and cuff. Basic pattern given below can be varied as desired. The number of rows in each part of the doll can be increased or decreased to suit individual designs. Garter stitch can be used to vary the texture.

*Abbreviations:* K—*knit*; P—*purl*; st(s)—*stitch(es)*; cont—*continue*; tog—*together*; st st—*stocking stitch*; inc—*increase*; dec—*decrease*; sc—*single crochet*; ch—*chain*; rep—*repeat*; alt—*alternate*; foll—*following*; beg—*beginning*; patt—*pattern*.

## BOY

Cast on 34 sts for cuff. Knit 6 rows. Change to trouser colour and st st 16 rows. Knit 2 rows in contrast colour for belt. Change to jumper colour and st st 10 rows. Work 2 rows st st in contrast colour for neckband. Change to face colour.

*1st row:* K6, K2 tog, K18, K2 tog, K6 (32 sts). St st next 9 rows. Change to bouclé wool for hair.

*1st row:* K1, inc next and foll 29 sts, K1 (62 sts). Knit 3 rows without shaping.

*5th row:* K1, (K2 tog, K1) 20 times, K1 (42 sts).

*6th and alternate rows:* Knit.

*7th row:* K2 tog, K1 to end of row (28 sts).

*9th row:* K2 tog 14 times (14 sts).

*11th row:* K2 tog 7 times (7 sts).

*12th row:* Knit. Cast off.

*Note:* If a thick bouclé wool is used for hair, increase every alternate stitch in first row of hair and knit 5th row without decreasing.

*Dear Little Dolls to Knit*

## Variations

**Overalls:** Follow basic pattern to 15th row of trousers.

*Last row:* P21, turn.

*Next row:* K8. Work 7 rows on these 8 sts continuing pattern, cast off. Pick up 8 sts at back of bib. Join in wool and complete last row of trousers. Change to jumper or belt colour and follow basic pattern to complete doll.

**Red check overalls—Trousers:** Follow basic pattern to last row of cuff.

*1st row:* *K2 red, K2 white, rep from * to end.

*2nd row:* *P2 red, P2 white, rep from * to end.

*3rd and 4th rows:* St st red. Rep these 4 rows 3 times. St st 3 rows keeping patt correct.

*Next row:* P21, turn.

*Next row:* K1 red, K2 white, K2 red, K2 white, K1 red, turn. Work 7 rows st st in correct patt, cast off. Pick up 8 sts at back of bib. Join in wool and complete last row of trousers. Follow basic pattern from belt to complete doll.

**Separate legs:** Cast on 17 sts and follow basic pattern to 10th row of trousers. Rep for other leg.

*11th row:* Knit across both legs to join. Follow basic pattern from 13th row of trousers to complete doll.

**Cap:** Complete face, change to cap colour and knit or rib 4 rows without shaping.

*5th row:* K1, K2 tog, K6, K2 tog, K10, K2 tog, K6, K2 tog, K1 (28 sts).

*6th and alt rows:* Purl.

*7th row:* K3, K2 tog, K4, K2 tog, K6, K2 tog, K4, K2 tog, K3 (24 sts).

*9th row:* K2 (K2 tog, K4) 3 times, K2 tog, K2 (20 sts).

*11th row:* K3 (K2 tog, K2) 3 times, K2 tog, K3 (16 sts).

*13th row:* K1 (K2 tog, K2) 3 times, K2 tog, K1 (12 sts).

*15th row:* K2 (K2 tog) 4 times, K2 (8 sts).

*17th row:* (K2 tog) 4 times (4 sts). Break wool, pull through remaining sts. Pull up tightly and secure.

# GIRL

To make base cast on 14 sts.

*1st row:* Knit.

*2nd and alt rows:* Purl.

*3rd row:* Inc every st (28 sts).

*5th row:* K2, (inc 1, K2) 8 times, inc 1, K1 (37 sts).

*7th row:* K2, (inc 1, K3) 8 times inc 1, K2 (46 sts).

Knit next 6 rows.

**Skirt:** St st next 16 rows. Change to colour for belt.

*1st row:* (K2 tog, K2) 11 times, K2 tog (34 sts).

*2nd row:* Knit. Change to colour for jumper and follow the basic pattern for body.

**Skirt variations—Blue/white check skirt:** Follow basic patt to beg of skirt.

*1st row:* *K2 blue, K2 white, rep from * to end.

*2nd row:* *P2 blue, P2 white, rep from * to end.

*3rd and 4th rows:* St st in blue. Rep these 4 rows 3 times, then follow basic patt for belt.

**Black/brown/white skirt:** Follow basic patt to beg of skirt. St st 2 rows each, black, brown, black, white (8 rows).

*9th row:* *K2 black, K2 white, rep from * to end.

*10th row:* *P2 black, P2 white, rep from * to end. Break off white and cont skirt in black.

**Green/red/white skirt:** Follow basic patt to beg of skirt. St st 2 rows each green, red, green, white (8 rows).

*9th row:* *K1 green, K1 white, rep from * to end. Break off white and cont skirt in green following basic patt.

**Fair Isle skirt:** Follow basic patt to make base of skirt. K2 tog once at beg of 1st row to reduce skirt to 45 sts. Work 1st and next 15 rows in st st, **following colour key** (*see Fig. 1, p. 68*).

**Belt:** *1st row:* (K2 tog, K2) 11 times, K2 (34 sts).

*2nd row:* Knit. Complete doll from jumper following the basic pattern for boy.

## To make up dolls

Weave a thread in face colour across first row of face on wrong side. Take thread to right side and leave. Using ends of wool, sew sides together to form back seam from top of head to cuff. Secure remaining threads. Fill head and draw up thread to form neck.

**Girl:** Fill body section making skirt wider at hemline. Continue sewing seam on base, draw up cast-on stitches and finish off. Using matching wool, form arms by back stitching through all layers from top of skirt to approximately four stitches from neck.

**Boy:** Fill body section and draw up cast-on row of cuff, stitch securely. Stitch arms as for girl and legs matching centre front with back seam to six stitches from waistline.

**Nose:** Secure a length of wool in face, three stitches below hair to one side of centre. Working from side to side under three knitted stitches pull up nose. Make stitches from side of nose to opposite side of nostril and pull up tightly. Take thread to back and finish off. Embroider eyes and other features such as buttons and collars to complete the dolls.

**Overalls:** Crochet sc around bib. Crochet braces in ch to cross at back and sew at waistline.

**Braces:** Crochet ch to fit from front waist over shoulder to cross at back. Make ch to join braces at front.

**Embroidered numbers:** Work a number in chain stitch then couching in same colour. Backstitch in contrast colour around sides, and couch for more depth of colour.

**Plaits:** Using tapestry needle and long lengths of wool, work loop stitches 12 cm long under welt of cap from side of face to back of head. Cut loops, divide each side into three sections and plait. Bind ends and trim.

**Tufted hair:** Work loop stitch below cap as for plaits, with stitches 3 cm long. Cut loops and trim hair to desired shape.

**Grandma's hair:** Work head in face colour following directions for cap beg 5th row. Work hair in sections using double thread in satin stitch. Work over peak of cap to form top knot.

**Pompon:** Make pompon same size as a machine bobbin and sew it to the cap.

### Dear Little Dolls to Knit

Follow our chart to organise your colours correctly

YELLOW  ORANGE  GREEN  PINK  PURPLE

FIG 1 FAIR ISLE SKIRT

*Dear Little Dolls to Knit*

*To Baby with Love — knitted mice, lambs and seals*

# To Baby with Love

DESIGNED BY GWEN MERRILL

Adorable little toys and playthings to knit, sew and crochet for a new arrival!

## SCULPTURED SOFT BALL
### (11 cm diam)

Scraps of white and red polka-dot fabric
polyester fibrefilling

1. Following instructions on p. 6, enlarge diagrams in Fig. 1 (*p. 73*) and make patterns for half circle and gusset in firm paper. A 5 mm seam allowance is included on the pattern.
2. Cut 12 half-circles in white and 12 gussets in polka-dot.

3. Fold one half-circle in half with edges matching, and clip curve at C, 4 mm to mark centre.
4. With right sides together stitch one side of gusset from A to C. With needle down, swivel fabric and sew gusset to B along other side.
5. Check that corner is firmly stitched, turn to right side. Fill. Turn in seam allowance at side and slip-stitch closed.
6. Repeat Steps 3-5 eleven times.
7. Sew 3 units together at straight edges to make a cluster. Make 4 clusters. Sew 3 clusters together at straight

edges to make a ball. Insert last cluster and sew to seam ends of adjacent clusters.

## GUINEA PIG
### (7 cm long)

12.5 cm-diam circle white fake fur fabric for head/body
scraps of felt
scrap of fabric for base
two 9 mm plastic animal safety eyes
polyester fibrefilling

*To Baby with Love — ball, pram mobile, guinea pig and rattle*

1. Following instructions on p. 6, enlarge diagrams in Fig. 2 (*p. 73*). Cut one body/head in fur, one base in cotton fabric, two ears and one nose in felt. A 5 mm seam allowance is included on body and base.
2. Turn 5 mm seam allowance on base to wrong side and baste.
3. Trim 5 mm of fur from outer edge of body circle. Mark position of eyes. Note that direction of fur runs backwards from nose. Pierce holes, trim small area of fur from right side.
4. Gather trimmed edge of circle. Pull up body to fit base. Secure thread.
5. Insert eyes, attach backs. Fill body softly, sew to base.
6. Gather straight edge of ear and sew above eye. Gather edge of circle for nose, insert small piece of filling. Sew at centre front below eyes. Sink eyes into head by stitching from side to side and pulling thread up tightly.

*Abbreviations:* K—*knit*; P—*purl*; st(s)—*stitch(es)*; cont—*continue*; tog—*together*; st st—*stocking stitch*; inc—*increase*; dec—*decrease*; ch—*chain*; dc—*double crochet*; rep—*repeat*; alt—*alternate*; foll—*following*; beg—*beginning*; patt—*pattern*.

## PRAM MOBILE
*(Doll's height 9 cm)*

Small quantities Sirdar Fontein Crepe
  4-ply in red and white for body
small quantity Sirdar Style 10-ply
  bouclé in red for hair
1 pr 2.75 mm (No. 12) knitting needles
1 metre 2.5 cm wide red ribbon
46 cm 5 mm wide elastic
red sewing thread
tapestry needle
polyester fibrefilling
three 15 mm bells

The dolls are knitted in one piece with seam at centre back. arms worked separately. The purl side is the right side.

## Doll (make 3)

**Legs:** Cast on 16 sts in red. St st 5 rows. Break off yarn, leave sts on needle. Cast on 16 sts on other needle, st st 5 rows, do not break off yarn.
*Next row: Join legs:* Purl across both legs (32 sts).
**Body:** Join in white.
*1st and 2nd rows:* Purl.
*3rd row:* Knit.
*4th row:* Purl.
Change colour and rep these 4 rows three times keeping stripes correct. Break off red.
**Face:** Change to white.
*1st row:* P3 (P2 tog, P4) 4 times, P2 tog, P3 (27 sts).
*2nd and 3rd rows:* Knit. St st 6 rows ending knit row.
**Hair:** Join in bouclé. Knit 2 rows. St st 4 rows.
*Next row:* P2 (P2 tog, P1) 8 times, P1 (19 sts).
*Next row:* K1 (K2 tog) 9 times (10 sts).
*Next row:* (P2 tog) 5 times (5 sts).
*Next row:* K1 (K2 tog) twice (3 sts). Cast off.
**Arm** *(make 2):* Cast on 12 sts in red. St st 6 rows.
*7th row:* K2 tog across row (6 sts). Cast off.

## To make up

Weave white thread across first row of face on wrong side. Leave ends on right side. Sew sides of legs and gather up cast-on edges. Sew back seam to neck. Fill legs and body. Pull up neck and secure. Fill head and sew back opening. Sew arm seam, fill softly, sew to body at sides. Embroider eyes and mouth in red. Using bouclé and tapestry needle loop three 20 cm lengths of yarn at top of head, to make six 10 cm strands. Divide into 3 pr, plait to end and sew across. Using 3 strands red yarn weave from end to halfway along plait, sew through bell.

To make casing for elastic fold ribbon in half with right side outside. Mark centre and 15 cm each side for dolls. Machine sew edges together securing plait for each doll. Insert elastic, turn in ends of ribbon and machine sew across.

## STICK RATTLE
### *(18 cm long)*

Small quantities red, navy and white Patons Bluebell crepe 5-ply yarn
3.00 mm (No. 11) crochet hook
one 16 mm and six 13 mm bells

18 cm piece of 10 mm-diam dowel
tapestry needle
**Handle:** Using red 2 ch, 5 dc into 1st ch. Sl st into 1st dc to join round.
*Next rnd:* Work 2 dc into each dc until 10 dc.
Work even on 10 dc until dowel is covered when inserted in crochet. Sl st into every other dc until opening is closed. Break off yarn.
**Covered bells, small size** *(make 6):* * 2 ch, 5 dc into 1st ch. Sl st into 1st dc to join round.
*Next rnd:* Work 2 dc into each dc until 12 dc. Work even for 3 rnds. Insert bell. Work 1 dc into every other dc, 6 times. Sl st opposite last dc to close opening. Do not break off yarn. Work 9 ch, attach to crochet covered dowel at top with 2 sl sts. Work another 9 ch, sl st into crochet at start of first 9 ch. Fasten off. Using tapestry needle darn in yarn end securely.* Rep from * to * 5 times in selected colours, attaching bells at opposite points at top.
**Large bell** *(at top):* 2 ch, 5 dc into 1st ch. Sl st into 1st dc to join rnd.
*Next rnd:* Work 2 dc into each dc until 14 dc. Work even for 4 rnds. Insert bell. Work 1 dc in every other dc 7 times. Sl st opposite last dc to close.

## KNITTED MICE
### *(Height 14 cm)*

One each blue (B) and white (W) 25 g balls Sirdar Fontein crepe 4-ply
three 2.75 mm (No. 12) knitting needles
2.00 mm (No. 14) crochet hook
polyester fibrefilling
tapestry needle for sewing seams

The mice are knitted in one piece with a seam at the back. The skirt is knitted in at the waist. The arms and ears are sewn on after the animal has been sewn and filled.

### Girl

**Leg** *(make two):* * Using B cast on 21 sts for shoe. Knit 6 rows.
*7th row:* K6, K2 tog twice, K11 (19 sts).
*8th row:* Knit.
Change to W for stockings.
*9th row:* K5, K2 tog twice, K10 (17 sts).
*10th row:* Purl. Change colour for stripe.
*11th row:* K5, K2 tog, K10 (16 sts).
*12th row:* Purl.
St st 10 rows keeping stripes correct *. Break off yarn, leave sts on needle. Rep from * to * for second leg working 7th, 9th and 11th rows in reverse. Do not break off yarn.

*Next row:* Knit across both legs (32 sts). Keeping stripes correct st st 11 rows ending purl row. Leave sts on needle.
**Skirt:** Cast on 64 sts in blue. Knit 3 rows. Purl 1 row.
*5th row:* * K3 B, K2 W, * rep from * to * across row ending K4 B.
*6th row:* P3 B, * P4 W, P1 B * rep from * to * across row ending P2 B.
St st 9 rows in W ending K row.
*16th row:* P2 tog across row (32 sts). Leave sts on needle.
**Join skirt to body:** Hold body with skirt at front in left hand. Knit together one st from each needle in blue. St st 7 rows for jumper.
** *Next row—shape neck:* K2, (K2 tog, K1) 10 times (22 sts).
**Head:** Change to W, P10, P2 tog, P10 (21 sts).
*Next row:* K5, inc once in next st, K4, K3 times in next st, K4, inc once in next st, K5 (25 sts).
*Next and alt rows:* Purl.
*Next row:* K5, inc once in next st, K6, K3 times in next st, K6, inc once in next st, K5 (29 sts).
Cont to inc in same manner in following knit rows until 37 sts.
St st 3 rows without shaping.
*Next row:* K15, K2 tog, K3, K2 tog, K15 (35 sts).
*Next and alt rows:* Purl.
*Next row:* K13, K2 tog, K5, K2 tog, K13 (33 sts).
Cont to dec in same manner until 27 sts rem.
Purl one row.
*Next row:* K2 tog across row, K1 (14 sts).
*Next row:* P2 tog across row (7 sts).
*Next row:* K2 tog across row, K1 (4 sts).
*Next row:* K2 tog twice. Fasten off. **

**Arm** *(make 2):* Cast on 12 sts in B, st st 10 rows.
Change to W and st st 4 rows.
*Next row:* K2 tog across row (6 sts).
*Next row:* P2 tog across row (3 sts).
*Next row:* K3 tog. Fasten off.

**Ear** *(crochet 2):* Using 2.00 mm hook and W, ch 2.
*1st row:* 5 dc into 1st ch, 1 ch, turn.
*2nd row:* 2 dc in each dc (10 dc), 1 ch, turn.
*3rd row:* 2 dc in each dc (20 dc), turn.
*4th row:* Sl st in 2nd dc, 1 dc in next 16 dc, sl st in next dc. Fasten off.

### Boy

**First leg:** * Using B cast on 21 sts for shoe. Knit 6 rows.

*7th row:* K6, K2 tog twice, K11 (19 sts).
*8th row:* Knit.
*9th row:* Join in W for check patt: K2 W, sl 1 B, K2 W, sl 1 B, K2 tog twice W, (sl 1 B, K2 W) 3 times (17 sts).
*10th row:* P2 W, (sl 1 B, P2 W) 5 times.
*11th row:* Knit B.
*12th row:* Purl B.
Work 10 rows without dec keeping check patt correct * break off yarn. Leave sts on needle.
**Second leg:** Rep from * to * working 7th and 9th rows in reverse.
Do not break off yarn.
*Next row—join legs:* K16, K2 tog, K16 (33 sts).
*Next row:* P15, P2 tog, P16 (32 sts).
Work 10 rows keeping check patt correct. Break off W.
*Next row:* Knit B.
*Next row—belt loops:* P2, (sl 1, P2) 10 times.
*Next row:* K2 (sl 1 K2) 10 times. St st 9 rows in B for jumper.
Complete head following patt for Girl from ** to **.

## To make up

**Girl:** Weave a draw thread across first row of face on wrong side. Using ends of wool sew side then sole seam of shoe. Note that the position of inside leg seam is near the back of the foot along sole seam. Sew leg seam, then centre back seam to neck. Sew skirt seam. Fill feet, legs and body using small pieces of filling to define shaping. Fill head and pull up neck. Sew back head seam inserting more filling if necessary. Position ears and sew firmly. Embroider facial features in satin st following **photograph on p. 69. Sew arm seams, fill softly and sew to body.**
**Boy:** Sew inside leg seams and back seam from right side alternating colour of yarn to match checks. Make a twisted cord for belt. Thread at waist, knot ends.

# LAMB
### (Height 13 cm)

One ball Villawool Tundra bouclé yarn 14-ply for body
small quantities Villawool superwash 8-ply yarn in contrast colour for face and feet
1 pr 3.00 mm (No. 11) and 1 pr 4.50 mm (No. 7) knitting needles
1 pr 9 mm animal safety eyes
polyester fibre filling
tapestry needle for seams

30 cm, 4 mm wide ribbon and bell for decoration only

The body and face are worked in st st in one piece beginning at tail. Legs, ears and tail are sewn on later. The white lamb uses reverse side of stocking stitch. The face and feet of the blue lamb are worked on the right side, the body on the reverse.

## White lamb

**Body:** Using 4.50 mm needles and bouclé cast on 11 sts.
*1st row:* Inc in each st (22 sts). St st 19 rows. *21st row:* K10, inc in next st, K11 (23 sts).
*22nd row:* P2 tog, P9, K3 times in next st, P9, P2 tog (23 sts). *23rd row:* K2 tog, K9, K3 times in next st, K9, K2 tog, (23 sts). *24th row:* Rep 22nd row.
*25th row:* Rep 23rd row. *26th row:* Rep 22nd row. *27th row:* K2 tog, K3, (inc 1, K1) 3 times, K3 times in next st, (K1, inc 1) 3 times, K3, K2 tog(29 sts).
*28th row:* P2 tog, P25, P2 tog (27 sts).
*29th row:* K2 tog, K23, K2 tog (25 sts).
*30th row:* Purl.
**Face:** Change to 3.00 mm needles and blue 8-ply yarn.
*1st row:* P6, (P2 tog) 3 times, P1 (P2 tog) 3 times, P6 (19 sts).
*2nd row:* Purl (*Note:* Omit this row for purl fabric face.) St st 4 rows.
*7th row:* K4 (K2 tog) twice, K3, (K2 tog) twice, K4 (15 sts). St st 5 rows.
*13th row:* K1 (K2 tog) 3 times, K1, (K2 tog) 3 times, K1. Cast off.
**Leg** * (make 4): Using 3.00 mm needles and blue 8-ply, cast on 6 sts.
*1st row:* Inc in each st (12 sts). St st 4 rows*.
*6th row:* Change to 4.50 mm needles and bouclé, (K2 tog) 6 times (6 sts).
*7th row:* Knit.
St st 6 rows. Cast off loosely.
**Tail:** Using 4.50 mm needles and bouclé cast on 3 sts.
*1st row:* Inc in each st (6 sts).
St st 4 rows. Cast off loosely.
**Ear** (make 2): Using 4.50 mm needles and bouclé, cast on 3 sts.
Cast off 3 sts. Break off yarn.
Pull yarn gently to remove bouclé loops. With tapestry needle, overcast edge of ear to cast-on edge, pull into triangle shape.

## Blue lamb

**Body:** Work as for white lamb omitting 2nd row (purl) of face.
**Leg:** Work from * to * of White lamb in white 8-ply.

*6th row:* Change to 4.50 mm needles and blue bouclé (P2 tog) 6 times (6 sts).
*7th row:* Knit.
St st 6 rows. Cast off loosely.

## To make up

With right sides inside, using tapestry needle and yarn ends, gather cast-off edge of nose. Sew head seam. Change yarn and continue to sew under body seam. Leave body open at end for filling. Turn to right side. Position eyes between decrease sts on face and attach safety backs. Insert small pieces of filling in nose, face and head shaping. Fill body softly. Sew opening closed. Sew tail seam, turn to right side and fold in half with seam underneath at centre. Do not fill. Sew with both cast-off edges together at tail. Gather cast-on edge of leg, sew seam. Turn to right side and fill. Sew close to underbody seam at front and back. Sew cast-on edge of ears to head above eyes. Tie ribbon and bell around neck for decoration only.

# SEAL
### (Length 21 cm)

25 (along pile) × 30 cm wide piece white fur fabric
two 12 mm plastic animal safety eyes
polyester fibrefilling bell
or rattle (use a small plastic tablet tube containing stones and sealed with tape)
1. **Following instructions on p. 6, enlarge diagrams in Fig. 3 (p. 73). Note** pattern markings and direction of pile. A 5 mm seam allowance is included.
2. Mark in pencil on wrong side of fur, noting direction of pile, one pair side body pieces, and one each underbody and head gusset. Using sharp pointed scissors cut through backing fabric only. Do not cut pile. Trim 5 mm fur from all edges.
3. With right sides together sew head gusset to side body pieces from A to B. Sew centre back seam from B to C. Sew seams twice with right sides together. Sew side body to underbody from A to C on both sides pushing fur inside body with point of scissors as you sew. Leave opening on one side only. Trim corners, clip curves. Pierce holes for eyes. Turn to right side and push out body shape with blunt instrument. Check position of eyes, trim fur and attach backs. Insert small pieces of filling into head and flippers until shape is well defined. Fill body softly. Insert rattle, close opening.

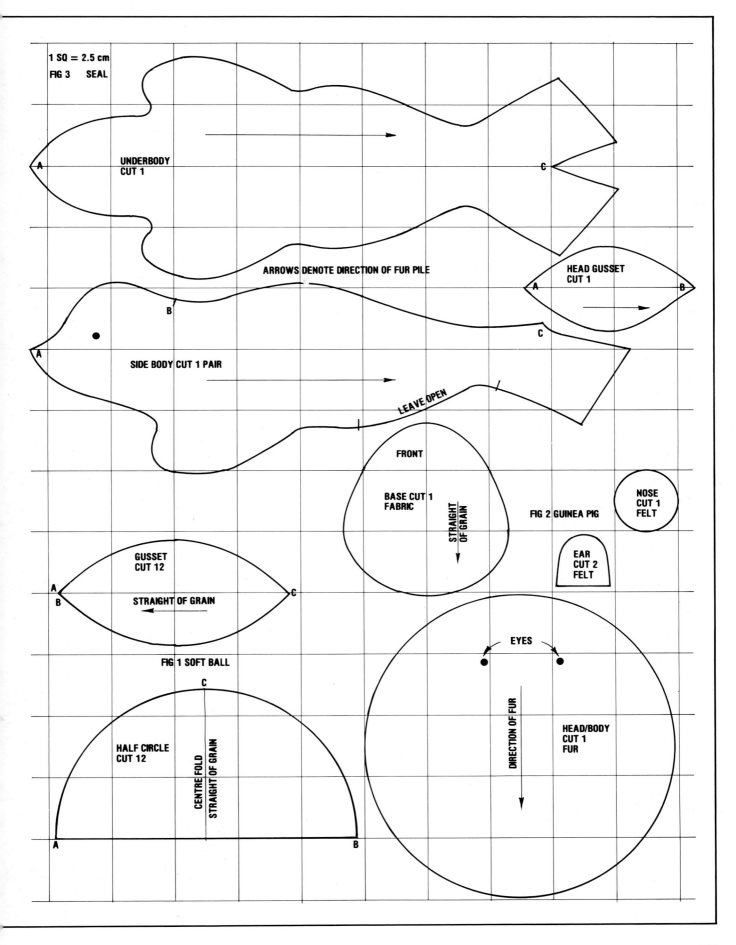

1 SQ = 2.5 cm
FIG 3    SEAL

UNDERBODY
CUT 1

A

C

ARROWS DENOTE DIRECTION OF FUR PILE

HEAD GUSSET
CUT 1

A

B

C

B

A

SIDE BODY CUT 1 PAIR

LEAVE OPEN

FRONT

BASE CUT 1
FABRIC

STRAIGHT
OF GRAIN

FIG 2 GUINEA PIG

NOSE
CUT 1
FELT

GUSSET
CUT 12

A

B

C

STRAIGHT OF GRAIN

EAR
CUT 2
FELT

FIG 1 SOFT BALL

EYES

DIRECTION OF FUR

HEAD/BODY
CUT 1
FUR

C

HALF CIRCLE
CUT 12

CENTRE FOLD
STRAIGHT OF GRAIN

A

B

# Life-size Playmates

DESIGNED BY GWEN MERRILL

## A boy doll and a girl doll you can dress in your children's old clothes! (Height 118 cm.)

*For one doll*
280 × 90 cm wide calico for body
one hank coloured macramé jute for hair
2-3 kg polyester fibre filling
length of narrow tape (*optional*)
length of ribbon for plaits
red, black felt-tip pens for face
sewing thread
*Dress*
1.3 × 90 cm wide printed cotton
five 3 cm buttons
matching thread
*Note:* Dress fits size 4-5 and measures 54 cm from centre back to hem, plus 3 cm hem.

### To make patterns
Two methods for making doll are given as follows.
*Method 1:* Place newspaper on floor and pose child with limbs slightly extended, feet straight. Trace around body and make an allowance for length of foot.

Adjust pattern, making calf and thigh muscles thicker. Fold pattern in half lengthwise to make symmetrical and cut out allowing 6 mm for seams. Mark ankle dart for front foot approximately 5 cm at widest part (*see Fig. 1*).
*Method 2:* Enlarge doll and dress patterns (*see Figs. 1 and 2, p. 76*), following directions given on p. 6.

A 6 mm seam allowance is included on all pattern pieces.

### To make body
1. Cut two body pieces, mark ankle dart on front foot only. Fold and stitch dart on wrong side.
2. Place body pieces together, sew around with a small stitch twice, leaving open at one side for the stuffing as marked.
3. Zigzag over raw edges and clip curves. Sharp curves such as thumbs, neck, armpit and between legs can be reinforced by stitching a length of

narrow tape or half strip of bias binding along stitching line. Turn to right side.
4. Press hands and feet, mark stitching line for fingers and toes with chalk. Machine and reverse stitch at both ends.
5. To stuff use several small pieces of filling for each toe or finger and insert with blunt pencil or crochet hook.
6. Stuff rest of doll using a ruler to assist in packing firmly.
7. The legs and arms can be stitched at the joints, using a zipper foot before stuffing head and body.

The head and neck require extra firm stuffing. Topstitch opening securely.

### Boy's hair
1. Wrap yarn closely around a ruler and hand sew securely along one side. Slide ruler out, twist coils to obtain curly effect. Repeat this five or six times.
2. Arrange lengths of curls on head in random way, or coil from centre top with rows approximately 1 cm apart. Attach to head firmly with several stitches every 6 mm.

### Girl's hair
1. Wrap yarn around a box approximately 50 cm long and 2.5 cm deep. Topsew securely across the centre of one end of box to a width of 20 cm. Cut yarn at other end.
2. Fold yarn in half at stitched end and machine across strands close to hand stitching several times for extra firmness.
3. Pin hair across centre of head, starting 3 cm down on face from head seam. Stitch very firmly to head using double thread.
4. Divide each side into three sections and plait. Enclose ends in strong elastic bands and tie with ribbons. Trim ends evenly.
5. To ensure that strands of hair cover fabric head, stitch across halfway between centre part and beginning of

plait with concealed stitches. Secure hair firmly to head underneath the start of the plait.

### Face
Practise drawing faces on scrap calico. Some felt pens tend to run into the fabric. This can be prevented by coating calico with a spray fabric shield before commencing. Sketch face in lightly on doll with chalk before using felt pens.

### To make dress
1. Fold fabric in half lengthwise and place pattern pieces following layout (*see Fig. 2*).
2. Cut two backs, one front (*on fold*), two front yokes, four back yokes, one neck frill, two armhole frills and two 2 × 25 cm bias strips for armhole facings.
3. Fold neck frill in half lengthwise with right side inside and stitch across ends. Turn to right side, press and gather 6 mm from raw edges.
4. With right sides together sew across back and front shoulder seams of yoke and yoke facings, press open.
5. Gather frill and sew to neck edge of yoke, leaving 6 mm seam allowance on yoke at back opening.
6. With right sides together stitch skirt back and fronts down side seams and neaten seam edges.
7. Double machine neaten one side of each armhole frill. With right sides together stitch short ends to front and back armholes.
8. With right sides together stitch facings around armhole. Trim seams and press facing to wrong side. Fold under 6 mm and slipstitch.
9. Press back skirt facings to wrong side and neaten edges.
10. Gather entire skirt section including frills from centre back to centre back. With right sides together sew skirt and frills to yoke, leaving a 6 mm seam allowance on back yoke and matching dots on yokes with frill seams.
11. With right sides together, sew yoke facing to yoke around neck edge and down back opening. Trim corners and nick neck edge. Turn to right side and press. Turn under 6 mm on facing and slipstitch to back of yoke.
12. Make buttonholes as marked and sew on buttons. Turn up 1 cm then 3 cm for hem and slipstitch around.

### To dress boy doll
Use outgrown jeans and a T-shirt or some other bright coloured clothing.

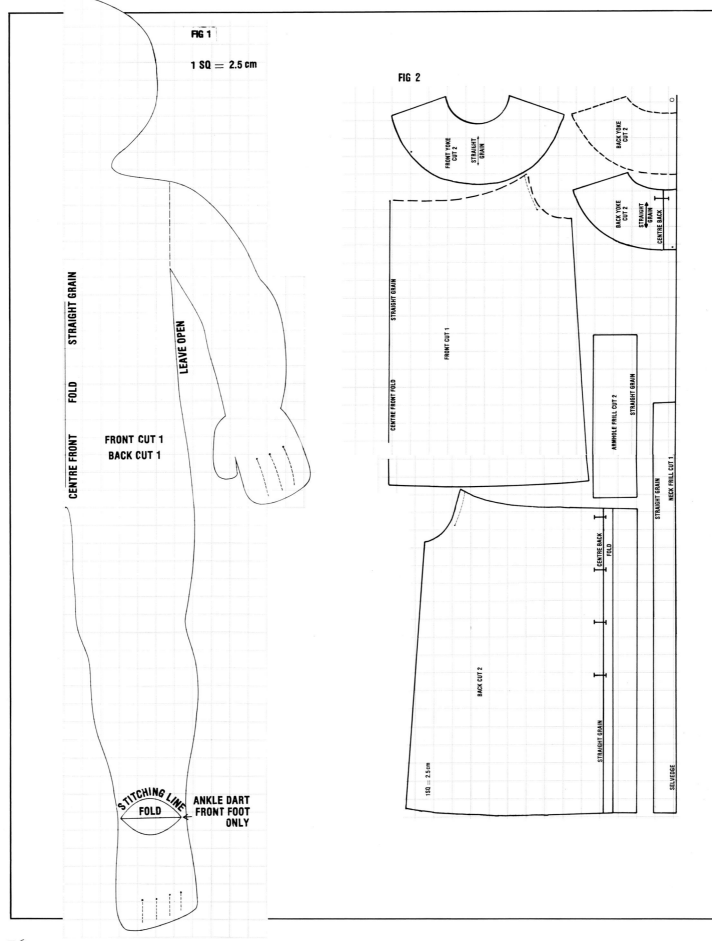

**FIG 1**

1 SQ = 2.5 cm

STRAIGHT GRAIN

FOLD

CENTRE FRONT

FRONT CUT 1
BACK CUT 1

LEAVE OPEN

STITCHING LINE
FOLD

ANKLE DART
FRONT FOOT
ONLY

**FIG 2**

FRONT YOKE
CUT 2

STRAIGHT
GRAIN

BACK YOKE
CUT 2

BACK YOKE
CUT 2

STRAIGHT
GRAIN

CENTRE BACK

STRAIGHT GRAIN

FRONT CUT 1

CENTRE FRONT FOLD

ARMHOLE FRILL CUT 2

STRAIGHT GRAIN

STRAIGHT GRAIN

NECK FRILL CUT 1

CENTRE BACK

FOLD

BACK CUT 2

STRAIGHT GRAIN

1SQ = 2.5 cm

SELVEDGE

*Tiny Treasures*

# Tiny Treasures

DESIGNED BY GWEN MERRILL

Brother-and-sister bears, pandas and pigs to knit.
They stand 15 cm tall.

The legs, body and head are knitted in one piece with a seam up the back. The arms and ears are sewn on after the animal has been filled.

Small quantities Patons Bluebell crepe 5-ply wool
three 2.75 mm (No. 12) knitting needles
2.00 mm (No. 7) crochet hook
polyester fibre for filling
1 pr 10 mm animal eyes for each bear
1 pr 8 mm plastic eyes for each pig
scraps of black felt for pig and panda
eyes
glue
black wool for noses and mouths
tapestry needle for sewing seams
black sewing thread

*Abbreviations:* K—*knit*; P—*purl*; st(s)—*stitch(es)*; cont—*continue*; tog—*together*; st st—*stocking stitch*; inc—*increase*; dec—*decrease*; sl st—*slip stitch*; psso—*pass slip stitch over*; ch—*chain*; dc—*double crochet*; rep—*repeat*; alt—*alternate*; foll—*following*; beg—*beginning*; patt—*pattern*.

## GIRL PANDA, BEAR AND PIG

### Legs (make two)

* Cast on 21 sts for shoe. Knit 6 rows.
*7th row:* K6, K2 tog twice, K11 (19 sts).
*8th row:* Knit.
*9th row:* Change colour for stockings. K5, K2 tog twice, K10 (17 sts).
*10th row:* Purl.
*11th row:* Change colour for stripes. K5, K2 tog, K10 (16 sts).
*12th row:* Purl.
St st 10 rows keeping stripes correct*. Break off yarn. Place sts on holder. Rep from * to * for 2nd leg, working 7th, 9th and 11th rows in reverse. Do not break off yarn.
*Next row:* K across both legs (32 sts)**. Cont in st st for 11 rows, ending purl row. Leave sts on needle. Put aside.

### Skirt

**Pig:** Cast on 64 sts in red. Knit 3 rows. Purl 1 row.
*5th row:* * K3 red, K2 pink *, rep from * to * across row ending K4 red.
*6th row:* P3 red, * P4 pink, P1 red *, rep from * to * across row ending P2 red.
St st 9 rows in pink ending knit row.
*16th row:* P2 tog across row in purple (32 sts).

**Bear:** Cast on 64 sts in purple. Knit 3 rows.
*4th row:* P2 purple, * P1 pink, P1 purple *, rep from * to * across row.
*5th row:* K1 purple, * K1 pink, K1 purple *, rep from * to * across row.
*6th row:* Purl 1 row purple.
*7th and 8th rows:* St st in pink.
*9th row:* Knit 1 row red.
St st 6 rows in pink, ending knit row.
*16th row:* P2 tog across row (32 sts).

**Panda:** Cast on 64 st in navy. Knit 2 rows.
*3rd row:* Knit 1 row orange.
*4th row:* * P1 navy, P1 orange *, rep from * to * across row.
*5th row:* Knit 1 row navy.
*6th row:* Work 4th row.
St st 9 rows in orange ending knit row.
*16th row:* P2 tog across row in navy (32 sts). Work following row in navy.

### To join skirt to body

Hold body with skirt at front in left hand. Knit together one st from each needle in jumper colour for bear, belt colour for panda and pig (32 sts).

## Jumper

St st 7 rows.

*Next row—shape neck:* K2, * K2 tog, K1 *, rep from * to * across row (22 sts).

## Head

**Bear and Panda:** * Join in brown/white, P10, P2 tog, P10 (21 sts).

*Next row:* K5, inc once in next st, K4, K3 in next st, K4, inc once in next st, K5 (25 sts).

*Next and alt rows:* Purl.

*Next row:* K5, inc once in next st, K6, K3 in next st, K6, inc once in next st, K5 (29 sts).

Cont to inc in same manner in foll K rows until 37 sts.*

St st 5 rows without shaping.

*Next row:* K16, cast off 5 sts, K16 (32 sts).

St st 5 rows without shaping.

*Next row:* K4, K2 tog, K8, K2 tog twice, K8, K2 tog, K4 (28 sts).

*Next row:* Purl.

*Next row:* K4, K2 tog, K6, K2 tog twice, K6, K2 tog, K4 (24 sts).

*Next row:* Purl.

*Next row:* K2 tog, across row (12 sts).

*Next row:* P2 tog, across row (6 sts).

*Next row:* K2 tog, across row (3 sts).

*Next row:* P3 tog. Fasten off.

**Pig:** Work from * to * of Bear's head. Purl next and alt rows.

*Next row:* K18, K3 into next st, K18 (39 sts).

*Next row:* K18, make 1, K3, make 1, K18 (41 sts).

*Next row:* K18, slip 1, K1, psso, K1, K2 tog, K18 (39 sts).

*Next row:* P18, slip 2 purlwise, slip first st over, sl st back on to left hand needle, P2 tog, P18 (37 sts).

*Next row:* K17, slip 2, slip first st over, sl st back on to left hand needle, K2 tog, K17 (35 sts).

Cont to dec in same manner in foll purl and knit rows until 29 sts rem.

*Next row:* K4, K2 tog, K17, K2 tog, K4 (27 sts).

*Next and alt rows:* Purl.

*Next row:* K4, K2 tog, K15, K2 tog, K4 (25 sts).

*Next row:* K4, K2 tog, K13, K2 tog, K4 (23 sts).

Work 2 sts tog in next and foll rows until 3 sts rem. K3 tog. Fasten off.

## Ears (crochet two)

**Panda and Bear:** * ch 2, 5 dc in 2nd ch from hook, 1 ch, turn.

*2nd row:* 2 dc in each dc (10 dc)*. Fasten off.

**Pig:** Work from * to * of Panda ear. Turn.

*3rd row:* Miss first dc, sl st in 2nd dc, 1 dc in foll 6 dc, sl st in next dc, turn.

*4th row:* Sl st in next dc, 1 dc in foll 3 dc, sl st in next dc, turn.

*5th row:* Sl st in next dc, 1 dc, sl st in next dc, turn.

*6th row:* Work 1 dc. Fasten off.

Using a tapestry needle and same colour, overcast row ends to neaten side edges.

## Arms

Cast on 12 sts and st st a total of 12 rows in desired colours. Change to head colour and st st 4 rows. Work 2 tog in foll rows until 3 sts rem. K3 tog. Fasten off.

## Bib

**Panda and Bear:** Pick up 8 sts across front and st st 6 rows. Cast off.

# BOY PANDA, BEAR AND PIG

Work in plain or pattern, from * to ** of Girl. Cont in st st for 10 rows ending knit row.

## Bib

*Next row:* P20, turn.

*Next row:* K8, turn. St st 5 rows. Cast off.

Pick up 8 sts behind bib in same colour with left hand needle. Purl 20 sts. Break off yarn. Join in colour for jumper, st st 12 rows keeping stripes correct.

*Next row:* K2, * K2 tog, K1 *, rep from * to * to end of row.

Complete **Head** foll directions for **Girl** as desired.

## Pig, checked pants

*1st and 2nd rows:* St st in yellow.

*3rd row:* K2 yellow, K2 pink, rep across row.

*4th row:* P2 pink, P2 yellow, rep across row.

Rep these 4 rows, commencing at the 9th row of directions for **Girl's legs.**

## To make up

Weave a thread in colour of jumper across first row of head on wrong side. Take thread to right side and leave. Using ends of wool, sew side, then sole seam of shoe. *Note that the position of inside leg seam is near the back of the foot along sole seam.* Sew leg seams, then centre back up to neckline. Sew skirt seam.

Fill feet, legs and body, using small pieces of filling to define shaping. For bears, fill head and position plastic eyes. Remove filling and attach eyes to metal back, with black felt eye patch for panda between plastic eye and knitting. Fill head using balls of fibre to push out snouts and cheeks. Sew up back head seam inserting more filling if necessary. Draw up thread to form neck. Secure well.

Position ears and sew firmly. To define pig's snout, work buttonhole stitch in pink over shaping to form a circle. Glue plastic pig's eyes on to slightly larger circle of black felt, and sew to face with black sewing thread. Sew eyelash to overlap plastic eye on girl's face. Hand sew edge of eye patch to panda's face with black sewing thread.

Embroider facial features in black wool, following photograph.

Sew arm seams. Fill softly and sew to body. Work one row double crochet around bib. Crochet a ch for each strap to cross at back and sew at waistline.

*Tiny Treasures — girl panda and boy panda*

*Friends from the Country — dolls*

# Friends from the Country

Make some Friends from the Country — dolls, chickens (which double as cushions) and a lovable hen picture all make ideal gifts for bedrooms or even the kitchen.

## CHICKEN CUSHIONS

*For each of the larger cushions:*
Co-ordinated 115 cm wide fabrics—
  about 50 cm for front and back
25 cm for boxing and scraps for
  appliqués
25 cm of 45 cm wide fusible interfacing
polyester fibre filling

1. Following instructions on p. 6, **enlarge patterns** (*see Fig. 1, p. 80*).
2. Pin pattern to folded fabric and trace outer edges. Then cut 1 cm *outside the traced lines*, for cushion back and front. Cut matching interfacing and baste it to wrong sides of front and back. Without seam allowances, cut appliqués (eye, head, beak and wing) from fabric and also from fusible interfacing.

3. *Feathers:* Cut a pair of feathers on the bias (with arrow on straight grain of fabric). Stitch them right sides together, 5 mm from curved edges; turn right side out and press. Take a small pleat at bottom and baste.
4. Pin appliqués to cushion front leaving 1 cm seam allowance at cushion edges with fusible interfacing in between. (For the feathered wing, on large front chicken, slide straight edges of feathers in between, also.) Iron them to fuse, then zigzag.
5. Pin feathers (*see arrows in pattern*) to cushion front, right sides together.
6. *Boxing:* Cut a boxing strip (6 cm wide for small birds or 8.5 cm wide for large birds) 2.5 cm longer than the bird outline. Starting at bottom centre, pin boxing (leaving a 1 cm seam allowance

at each end) to cushion front, right sides together and edges even. Stitch opposite edge to cushion back, starting at the same place. Stitch together with a 1 cm seam, leaving a 10 cm opening.
7. Turn right side out, fill, and slip-stitch opening closed.

## HEN PICTURE

Assorted scraps of fabric for appliqués, polyester quilt
wadding and background fabric, each
  about 55 cm deep × 67.5 cm wide
plywood or hardboard 40 × 55 cm
frame (*optional*)

1. Following directions on p. 50, enlarge the pattern (*see Fig. 2, p. 80*). Trace a separate pattern for each

appliqué (up to the broken lines, which indicate overlapped fabric).

2. Cut out appliqués and pin them in place on to the background fabric following the photograph as a placement guide. With machine set for an open zigzag, baste along appliqué edges. With a wider, closed zigzag, stitch again over basting.

3. Smooth wadding over the board, taping the edges to the back. On top, spread the appliquéd fabric and staple the edges to the back. Hang framed or unframed.

# DOLLS

Unbleached calico and black fabric for dolls
scraps of fabric for clothes
polyester fibrefilling
hat elastic for bonnet
grosgrain ribbon for pants
press-studs and hooks

1. Following instructions on p. 6, enlarge patterns (*see Fig. 3, p. 80*), (5 mm *seams allowed*)

2. Cut 1 pair of calico bodies and 2 pairs of black legs for each doll. For girl cut 2 yokes (1 for lining), two 23 × 28 cm skirt pieces and two 15 × 10 cm sleeves. For boy, cut 2 pant and 2 shirt pieces, two 10 × 13 cm sleeves and the hat pieces (two each of 8 cm circle, 14 cm circle and 23 × 4 cm crown).

3. Except at lower edges, sew a pair of bodies together, clip curves and turn right side out. Except at top edges, sew each pair of legs together, then clip, turn and stuff. Fold leg edges so seams match at centre, then stitch across top.

4. Pin legs to lower front edge of body, raw edges even and toes to chest. Stitch. Fill body, turn in lower back edge and slipstitch over leg edges.

5. Centre yarn at girl's forehead and hand-sew a centre parting across it. Draw yarn down behind head and sew across loops (the rest of head is covered by bonnet). For boy's beard, cut an 8 × 13 cm piece of tissue paper, loop yarn back and forth across short width and stitch (across the loops) through the centre. Tear away the tissue and tack the stitching line across the chin.

## Dress

Sew yoke to yoke lining around neck and back edges. Clip curves, turn right side out and baste the two together along raw edges. Sew skirt to waist front, gathering a 28 cm edge to fit. Repeat at waist back, with CB yoke edges butted. Sew hook and eye to close neck. Seam a 15 cm edge of sleeve to yoke (and skirt sides) centred at yoke shoulder. Repeat. Stitch underarm and side seams. Narrowly hem the skirt and stitch two 3 mm tucks above hem. Gather wrist edges and bind.

## Bonnet

Cut 50 × 18 cm strip of fabric and sew at short ends to make a loop. At one long (brim) edge, turn under 5 cm and pin. Stitch 3 cm and 3.5 cm from edge, to make casing. At opposite edge, turn under 1 cm and stitch casing. Insert 13 cm piece of elastic in top casing, pull tight and tie. Insert 35 cm elastic in brim casing and tie to fit head.

## Boy's shirt

Sew shirt pieces together at centre back. Turn under front edges 3 mm and stitch. Bind neck edge with a 3 × 20 cm strip of fabric, turning in raw ends. Sew a 13 cm edge of sleeve to shirt, centred at shirt shoulder. Repeat. Stitch underarm and side seams. Gather wrist edges and bind. Sew press-studs to front edges.

## Pants

Sew each pant piece at inside edges. Sew two pieces together at crutch seam, leaving 5 cm open at centre back. Gather waist edge and bind. Sew hook at back edges. Hem pant legs. Sew ends of 2.5 cm length of ribbon under waistband to make suspender loop. Repeat then fasten a 23 cm ribbon through each loop, cross them in back and sew ends to inside of waistband.

## Boy's hat

Sew the two larger circles together, turn right side out and press. In the centre, draw a 6 cm wide circle. Top-stitch 3 mm apart, from brim to drawn circle. Cut a hole 3 mm inside the drawn circle and clip to the stitching. Stitch short ends of crown together to make a loop. Repeat, then baste them right sides out and edges even. Baste small circles together the same. Top-stitch both 3 mm apart, parallel to edges. Sew one edge of crown to opening in brim. Stitch the other edge to the small circle. Tie ribbon around crown.

**Friends from the Country**

FIG 1 CHICKEN CUSHIONS    1 SQ = 2.5cm

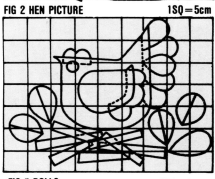

FIG 2 HEN PICTURE    1 SQ = 5cm

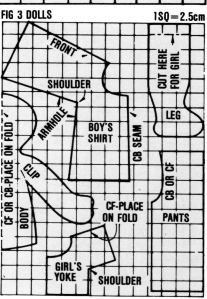

FIG 3 DOLLS    1 SQ = 2.5cm

*Friends from the Country — chicken cushions and hen picture*

# Friendly School Pigs to Knit

DESIGNED BY GWEN MERRILL

Everybody has a soft spot for pigs. These cute and cuddly school pigs, a boy and a girl, stand about 38 cm high.

Pigs are knitted in Paton's Totem 8-ply using 3.00 mm (No. 11) needles. Legs, body and head are knitted in one piece with seam at centre back. Arms, ears, tail and cap are worked separately.

Three 50 g balls Patons Totem in skin colour for both pigs
one ball each dark blue, light blue, orange and small quantities brown, red, yellow and beige
scraps of black, white and brown felt for eyes
black wool for nostrils and mouth
1 pr 3.00 mm (No. 11) and 2.75 mm (No. 12) knitting needles
3.00 mm (No. 11) crochet hook
tapestry needle for sewing seams
polyester fibre filling
seven 10 mm buttons for dress, jumper and bags
one 10 mm covered button for cap

*Tension:* 5 sts to 2 cm in width over stocking stitch.

*Abbreviations:* K—*knit;* P—*purl;* st(s)—*stitch(es);* cont—*continue;* tog—*together;* st st—*stocking stitch;* dec—*decrease;* inc—*increase;* make 1—*pick up loop between sts on left hand needle and knit into back of loop;* yfwd—*yarn forward;* ybk—*yarn back;* sl st—*slip stitch;* psso—*pass slip stitch over;* ch—*chain;* dc—*double crochet;* rep—*repeat;* alt—*alternate;* foll—*following;* beg—*beginning;* patt—*pattern.*

## GIRL PIG

**Body**
**Trotter:** * Using 3.00 mm needles, cast on 8 sts in brown. Knit 2 rows.
*3rd row:* Inc in first st, K2, K3 in next st, K3, inc in last st (12 sts).
*4th and alt rows:* Knit.
*5th row:* Inc in first st, K4, K3 in next st, K5, inc in last st (16 sts).
*7th row:* Inc in first st, K6, K3 in next st, K7, inc in last st (20 sts).
*9th row:* Inc in first st, K8, K3 in next st, K4, K3 in next st, K4, inc in last st (26 sts).
*11th row:* K18, K3 in next st, K7 (28 sts).
*13th row:* K19, K3 in next st, K8 (30 sts)**.
*14th row:* K18, yfwd, sl 1, Turn, yfwd, sl 1, ybk, K16, yfwd, sl 1, Turn, yfwd, sl 1, ybk, K to end of row. Knit 2 rows.

**Leg:** Change to pink.
*1st row:* K2 tog, K4, K2 tog, K4, K2 tog, K6, K2 tog, K6, K2 tog (25 sts). St st 3 rows.

**Heel** *5th row:* K13, K2 tog twice, K5 into next st, Turn, work 6 rows st st on these 5 sts, K2 tog twice, K3 (25 sts).
*6th row:* P4, P2 tog, P3, P2 tog, P14 (23 sts).
*7th row:* K13, K2 tog, K3, K2 tog, K3 (21 sts).
*8th row:* Purl ***.
St st 24 rows, break off yarn.

**Second leg:** Work from * to ** in reverse.

**Trotter** *14th row:* K28, yfwd, sl 1, Turn, yfwd, sl 1, K16, yfwd, sl 1, Turn, yfwd, sl 1, K to end of row. Knit 2 rows. Work 1st to 8th rows of leg in reverse. St st 24 rows.

**Join legs:** K20, make 1, K1,(next leg) K1, make 1, K20 (44 sts).
*2nd and 4th rows:* Purl.
*3rd row:* K19, make 1, K6, make 1, K19 (46 sts).
*5th row:* K18, make 1, K10, make 1, K18 (48 sts). St st 43 rows.

**Shape shoulders:** K11, K2 tog, K22, K2 tog, K11 (46 sts).
*Next and alt rows:* Purl.
*Next row:* K11, K2 tog, K20, K2 tog, K11 (44 sts). Cont to dec in same manner until 40 sts rem. Purl one row.
*Next row:* K11, K2 tog, K6, K2 tog, K6, K2 tog, K11 (37 sts). Purl one row. Tie markers at each end of row.

**Head** *1st row:* K11, make 1, K7, make 1, K1, make 1, K7, make 1, K11 (41 sts).
*2nd and alt rows:* Purl.
*3rd row:* K11, make 1, K9, make 1, K1, make 1, K9, make 1, K11 (45 sts). Cont to inc in this manner at side of head and for snout until 65 sts. Purl one row.

**Snout** *15th row:* K31, make 1, K3, make 1, K31 (67 sts).
*16th and alt rows:* Purl.
*17th row:* K31, make 1, K5, make 1, K31 (69 sts).
*19th row:* K31, sl 1, K1, psso, K3, K2 tog, K31 (67 sts).
*21st row:* K31, sl 1, K1, psso, K1, K2 tog, K31 (65 sts).
*22nd row:* P31, sl 1, P2 tog, psso, P31 (63 sts).
*23rd row:* K28, cast off 7, K28 (56 sts). St st 5 rows.
*29th row:* K10, sl 1, K1, psso, K2 tog, K12, sl 1, K1, psso, K2 tog, K12, sl 1, K1, psso, K2 tog, K10 (50 sts).
*30th and alt rows:* Purl.
*31st row:* K9, sl 1, K1, psso, K2 tog, K10, sl 1, K1, psso, K2 tog, K10, sl 1, K1, psso, K2 tog, K9 (44 sts).
*33rd row:* K8, sl 1, K1, psso, K2 tog, K8, sl 1, K1, psso, K2 tog, K8 sl 1, K1 psso, K2 tog, K8 (38 sts).
*35th row:* K7, sl 1, K1, psso, K2 tog, K6, sl 1, K1, psso, K2 tog, K6, sl 1, K1 psso, K2 tog, K7 (32 sts).
*37th and 39th rows:* K2 tog across row (8 sts). Cast off.
*Note:* Boy's body is 6 sts larger around waist. Increase shaping begins near top of legs, decrease shaping is completed above stomach.

# BOY PIG

## Body

Follow directions for Girl pig from *
(beginning) to *** (8th row of leg). St
st 20 rows.
*Next row:* K10, make 1, K11 (22 sts).
*Next row:* Purl.
*Next row:* K11, make 1, K11 (23 sts).
*Next row:* Purl, break off yarn. Work
second leg in reverse—see directions
for Girl pig.
Join legs: K11, make 1, K11, make 1,
K1 (second leg) K1, make 1, K11,
make 1, K11 (50 sts).
*Next and alt rows:* Purl.
*Next row:* K22, make 1, K6, make 1,
K22 (52 sts).
*Next row:* K21, make 1, K10, make 1,
K21 (54 sts). St st 27 rows.
*Next row:* K10, K2 tog, K30, K2 tog,
K10 (52 sts).
*Next and alt rows:* Purl.
*Next row:* K10, K2 tog, K28, K2 tog,
K10 (50 sts).
*Next row:* K10, K2 tog, K26, K2 tog,
K10 (48 sts). St st 11 rows.
Complete boy foll directions for Girl
pig from shape shoulders.

## Arm (make 2)

Using 3.00 mm needles, cast on 9 sts in
brown. Knit one row.
*Next row:* K1, inc 1 st in next 7 sts, K1.
(16 sts). Knit 6 rows.
Change to pink, st st 24 rows, inc at
both ends of 7th and 15th rows (20 sts).
Cast off 3 sts at the beg of next 4 rows
(8 sts). Cast off.

## Ear (crochet 2)

Ch 10, 1 dc in 2nd ch from hook, 3 dc,
work 3 dc in next dc, 4 dc, 1 ch, turn.
Work 2 rows in dc.
*4th row:* 4 dc, miss 1 dc, 1 dc, miss 1 dc,
4 dc, 1 ch, turn.
*5th and alt rows:* 1 dc in each dc, do not
ch to turn.
*6th row:* 3 dc, miss 1 dc, 1 dc, miss 1 dc,
3 dc.
*8th row:* 2 dc, miss 1 dc, 1 dc, miss 1 dc,
2 dc.
*10th row:* 1 dc, miss 1 dc, 1 dc, miss 1
dc, 1 dc.
*11th row:* 1 dc. Fasten off.

## To make up

Using matching yarn, weave across
neck at markers on wrong side leaving
ends on right side for pulling in neck.
Sew openings in heel shaping and at top
of snout. Sew foot, inside leg and centre
back seam to neck. Turn to right side.

To form trotter, stitch foot through
centre front and back from tip to last
shaping row on underside, leaving
extra rows on underside unstitched. Fill
each side of foot, legs, body and head.
Pull in neck and close head opening.

Working on the right side, buttonhole stitch in matching yarn over
shaping rows, to form a circle for end
of snout. Sew arm seams. Turn to right
side and stitch hand through centre. Fill
and sew arms to body at shoulder. Sew
ears to side of head below shaping line.
Embroider nostrils and mouth in black
following photograph. Cut felt eye
pieces (*see Fig. 1, page 85*), sew white
and brown sections to face with matching thread. Fold boy's eyelid in half and
sew over top half of eyeball leaving
folded edge unstitched. Sew girl's eyelid
leaving lashes unstitched.

## Dress

**Back skirt:** * Using 3.00 mm needles
cast on 54 sts in dark blue. Knit 4 rows.
**Check patterning:** Using light blue
(LB) and orange (O) work the following 4 rows, 8 times.
*1st row:* Knit (LB).
*2nd row:* Purl (LB).
*3rd row:* K1 (O), * sl 1 (LB), K2 (O) *
rep from * to * across row, sl 1 (LB),
K1 (O).
*4th row:* K1 (O), * sl 1 (LB), P2 (O) * rep
from * to * across row, sl 1 (LB), K1
(O).
*Note:* Press work on wrong side before
working next row.

**Bodice:** *Next row:* Work in LB, K1, K2
tog 26 times, K1 (28 sts)*.
St st 9 rows. Cast off 4 sts at the beg of
the next 2 rows (20 sts).
St st 6 rows.
*Next row, right side:* K6, turn.
*Next row:* P6. St st 8 rows. Cast off. Join
in yarn and cast off 8 sts for neck and
complete left side to correspond.

**Front:** Work as for Back from * to *.
Purl 1 row.
*Next row, right side:* K13, turn. St st 7
rows. Cast off 4 sts at the beg of the
next row. St st 6 rows.
*Next row:* Cast off 3 sts for neck, P6. St
st 8 rows. Cast off.
Join in yarn for left side, cast off 2 sts
at centre, K13. Complete to correspond
with right side.

## To make up

Sew side and shoulder seams. Overcast
slipped stitches at skirt edges together

from the right side. Starting at waist on left side front, using 3.00 mm crochet hook and dark blue, sl st around cast-off edge of front opening and neck. Work 1 dc into each sl st, making two 3 ch loops at centre and top of left side for buttonholes. Crochet around armholes in same manner. Sew on buttons.

## Knickers

Using 2.75 mm needles, cast on 28 sts. Work 4 rows in rib of K1, P1. Change to 3.00 mm needles and st st 12 rows. Cast off 4 sts at the beg of the next 6 rows (4 sts). St st 10 rows. Cast on 4 sts at beg of next 6 rows (28 sts). St st 12 rows. Change to 2.75 mm needles and rib 4 rows. Cast off in rib.

## To make up

Sew side seams. Using 3.00 mm crochet hook, sl st around cast-off edges of leg. For shell edge work * 2 dc, 3 ch, sl st in 1st ch * rep from * to * around leg.

## Jumper

**Front:** Using 2.75 mm needles cast on 34 sts. Work 4 rows in rib of K1, P1. Change to 3.00 mm needles and st st 22 rows, dec both ends of 9th and 15th rows (30 sts). Cast off 3 sts at the beg of next 2 rows, and 1 st each end of next row (22 sts). St st 9 rows.
*Next row:* K5, K2 tog, turn. Purl to end of row.
*Next row:* K4, K2 tog, (5 sts). St st 3 rows. Cast off.
Join in yarn, cast off 8 sts for neck, K7.
*Next row:* P5, P2 tog.
*Next row:* Knit.
*Next row:* P4, P2 tog (5 sts). St st 3 rows. Cast off.

**Back:** Work as for Front to 16th row. (30 sts).
*Next row:* K15, turn, purl to end of row. St st 4 rows.
*Next row:* Cast off 3 sts, K12.
*Next row:* Purl.
*Next row:* Cast off 1 st, K to end of row. St st 12 rows.
*Next row:* Cast off 6 sts for neck, P5.
*Next row:* K5. Cast off.
Join in wool and complete left side to correspond.

**Sleeves:** Using 2.75 mm needles cast on 26 sts and work 4 rows in rib. Change to 3.00 mm needles and st st 16 rows, inc both ends of 7th and 11th rows (30 sts). Cast off 3 sts at the beg of next 2 rows, and 1 st both ends of foll row. Purl one row. Cast off.

## To make up

Sew shoulder seams, then sleeve head to armhole. Sew underarm and side seams. Crochet in contrast colour around neck and back opening, see directions for Girl's dress, making a chain loop for buttonhole at neck.
*Letter:* Using yellow, crochet P in sl st on right side of jumper front. Back-stitch around both sides of letter in red, then couch the back stitches. Sew button at neck.

## Trousers

* Using 3.00 mm needles cast on 30 sts in yellow. Knit 4 rows. Work check pattern in orange and beige for 22 rows, see Girl's dress *. Rep from * to * for second leg.
*Next row:* Keeping patt correct join legs (60 sts). Purl one row.
*Next row:* K29, make 1, K2, make 1, K29 (62 sts).
*Next row:* P31, make 1, P31 (63 sts). Cont in check patt for 30 rows.
Change to 2.75 mm needles and work 4 rows rib in orange for waistband. Cast off.

## To make up

Overcast slipped stitches together at edges from right side. Sew inside leg then centre back seam.

## Cap

Using 3.00 mm needles, cast on 6 sts.
*1st row:* Inc in each st (12 sts).
*2nd row:* Inc 1 st, P10, inc 1 st (14 sts).
*3rd row:* K1 (inc 1, K1) 6 times, K1 (20 sts).
*4th and alt rows:* Purl.
*5th row:* K1 (inc 1, K2) 6 times, K1 (26 sts).
*7th row:* K1 (inc 1, K3) 6 times, K1 (32 sts).
Cont to inc in this manner until 50 sts. Work 1 row purl then 2 rows knit. Cast off.

**Peak:** Pick up 14 sts on cast-off edge at centre. Purl 1 row. K2 tog at both ends of every row until 4 sts rem, cast off.

## To make up

Using a tapestry needle, overcast cast-off edges of peak with ends of wool. Sew back seam. Fill cap and sew to boy's head. Sew button at top.

## School bag

Using 3.00 mm needles, cast on 14 sts. Inc both ends of next 2 rows (18 sts).

St st 38 rows. Cast on 4 sts both ends of next row (26 sts). Cont in st st for 20 rows, working a knit st at the 5th and 22nd st in every purl row. Cast off on purl row, do not break off yarn.

## To make up

Using a 3.00 mm crochet hook, sl st back 4 sts across cast-off edge. Crease bag along line of knit sts. Work in dc along this edge to beg of extension. Fold bag around extension and dc through both edges, across base and up side. Cont in dc around flap to other side. Join in extension on corresponding row and cont in dc along side, base and line of knit sts to cast-off edge. Fasten off. Crochet 2 chain loops on front edge of flap. Sew on buttons.
**Strap:** Using 2.75 mm needles, cast on 4 sts and knit strap length required to fit over clothing. Sew ends to back of bag at top.
**Handle:** Crochet a chain loop on top of flap. Work back in dc over chain, fasten off. Sew a press-stud to centre of handle and inside of hand.

**FIG 1 EYES — ACTUAL SIZE**

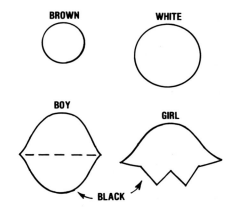

# Make a Friendly Panda

This great big furry panda, at about 66 cm tall, will stand almost as tall as a toddler. Furry and lovable, it may well become a favourite family friend.

80 × 150 cm wide white fur fabric
60 × 150 cm wide black fur fabric
two 23 cm squares black felt
275-350 g polyester fibre filling
two 18-30 mm diameter eyes or
 buttons
**Following directions on page 6, enlarge pattern page 88. Add 6 mm seam allowance around each piece, except Nos 4, 7, 14 and 15. Cut out.**

*Cutting note:* Cut one of each unless otherwise indicated. Pin patterns to wrong side of fur cloth, with arrow on the grain and pointing down the pile. When a pair is called for, turn the pattern over to cut one of the pieces, so that you get one right and one left to make the pair.

*White fur*
No. 1   Side Head (1 pair)
No. 3   Upper Head Gusset
No. 5   Lower Head Gusset
No. 6   Nose Gusset
No. 9   Body (1 pair)
No. 12 Lower Front Gusset

*Black fur*
No. 2   Ear (2 pairs)
No. 4   Eye Patch (1 pair)
No. 7   Nose Patch
No. 8   Upper Arm (1 pair)
No. 10 Leg (2 pairs)
No. 11 Upper Front Gusset
No. 13 Inner Arm (1 pair)

*Black felt*
No. 14 Sole (1 pair)
No. 15 Paw (1 pair)

*A Friendly Panda*

## To sew panda (6 mm seam allowance)

*Head:* Slipstitch an eye patch (4) to each side head (1). Cut out dart 6 mm from drawn lines (*do not sew dart*). With right sides together, stitch each pair of ears except at straight edges. Turn right side out. Stitch ear to side head, with ear seam over front stitching line of dart, starting 6 mm from the top edge; sew dart to enclose ear raw edges. With right sides together and ear facing forward, stitch upper head gusset (3) to side heads, matching A's and B's. Attach eyes (buttons, if used, can be sewn on after filling). With right sides together, stitch lower head gusset (5) to side heads, matching C's and D's. With right sides together, stitch nose gusset (6) to head, matching B's and C's. Slipstitch nose patch (7) to gusset.

*Body—back seams:* With right sides together, stitch upper arms (8) together at centre back seam, from E to F. With right sides together, stitch body (9) pieces together at centre back seam, from G to H. With right sides together, stitch upper arms (8) to body between O's, matching G to F and I to O. With right sides together and centre backs matching, pin head to upper arms between D's easing head to fit. Stitch. With right sides together, stitch outer part of each leg (10) to body, matching I's and J's.

*Front seams:* With right sides together, stitch upper front gusset (11) to lower front gusset (12), matching K's. With right sides together, stitch inner arms (13) to front gusset, matching L's and K's. With right sides together, stitch inside part of legs (10) to front gusset (12) matching I's and J's.

*Side seams:* Starting at H, with right sides together, stitch front to back, leaving opening between P and Q (*for sole*) and at front neck (*for filling*).

*Finishing:* Clip inside curves and corners. Turn head and body right side out. Stuff. Slipstitch head to body around neck opening. Turn in seam allowance at bottoms of legs. Pin and whipstitch edge of sole (14) to leg, adding filling, if necessary. Slipstitch paws (15) to inner arms.

1. SIDE HEAD
2. EAR
3. UPPER HEAD GUSSET
4. EYE PATCH
5. LOWER HEAD GUSSET
6. NOSE GUSSET
7. NOSE PATCH
8. UPPER ARM
9. MAIN BODY
10. OUTER/INNER LEG
11. UPPER FRONT GUSSET
12. FRONT GUSSET
13. INNER ARM
14. FOOT SOLE
15. PAW

## Make a Friendly Panda

Follow our chart at right to identify each pattern piece

WHITE FUR (NO SEAM ALLOWANCES)

DIRECTION OF PILE

BLACK FUR (NO SEAM ALLOWANCES)

DIRECTION OF PILE

STRAIGHT GRAIN

1 SQ = 5 cm
FELT

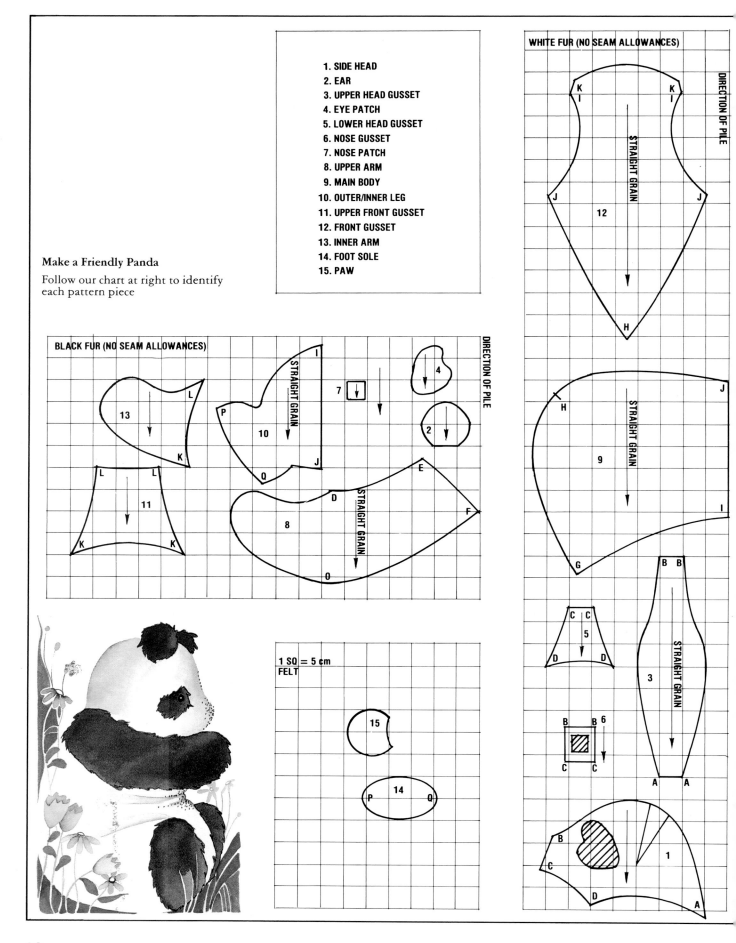

# Five Crazy Cushions

Fun cushions to make — an apple, a lion, a clown's head, a bear and a mouse.

*Five Crazy Cushions*

*Main colour felt: Apple*—23 × 50 cm; *Lion*—32 × 72 cm; *Clown (two shades)* and *mouse*—23 × 62 cm; *Bear*—32 × 72 cm

scraps coloured felt for facial features and ear linings

polyester fibre filling

quantity 4-ply yarn for pompons

fabric glue

1. Follow directions on p. 6, enlarge patterns and faces in Figs. 1–5 below. Cut out patterns. Trace off faces and ears, etc. on to separate pieces of paper to make separate patterns.
2. Using the photograph as a guide for colour, cut two cushion pieces (front and back), facial features, ear linings, apple worm holes, 5 cm square stems and apple leaves from felt.
3. Again using photograph as guide, glue cheeks and worm holes to cushion fronts and ear linings to ears. Sew on small pompons for eyes, clown hat trim and green worm, for noses (*pompon directions*). Stitch freckles with french knots and use backstitches for mouths and whiskers (*see p. 7 for stitches*).
4. For clown, lap and glue hat piece over head top edge to make one-piece front and back cushion pieces. With wrong sides together and edges even, handsew cushion front to back 6 mm from edges, leaving small opening for the stuffing; stuff them firmly.

5. *Ears:* All ears are sewn to back of seam in positions shown in photograph. For mouse, sew lined ear to ear back, stuff and sew ear to the cushion.
6. *Trims:* Sew large pompons around cushion as shown. Spread one side of apple stem piece with glue; roll up. Sew stem to apple top, along with leaves, as shown.

## Pompons

Cut 10 cm strips of cardboard in the following widths and yarn lengths as specified:

    2.5 cm small pompon, 5.5 m yarn

    4 cm medium pompon, 7.5 m yarn

    5 cm large pompon, 10 m yarn

Wind yarn firmly and overlapping, around cardboard. Tie wrapped yarn tightly at one edge with another short piece. Cut through yarn at opposite edge to remove cardboard. Fluff the yarn with your fingers into a ball shape and trim off any uneven ends.

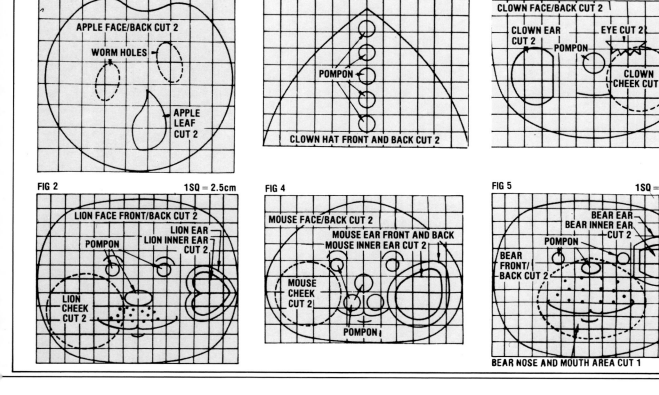

FIG 1 — NOVELTY CUSHIONS — 1SQ = 2.5cm — APPLE FACE/BACK CUT 2 — WORM HOLES — APPLE LEAF CUT 2

FIG 3 — 1SQ = 2.5cm — POMPON — CLOWN HAT FRONT AND BACK CUT 2

CLOWN FACE/BACK CUT 2 — CLOWN EAR CUT 2 — POMPON — EYE CUT 2 — CLOWN CHEEK CUT 2

FIG 2 — 1SQ = 2.5cm — LION FACE FRONT/BACK CUT 2 — POMPON — LION EAR LION INNER EAR CUT 2 — LION CHEEK CUT 2

FIG 4 — MOUSE FACE/BACK CUT 2 — MOUSE EAR FRONT AND BACK MOUSE INNER EAR CUT 2 — MOUSE CHEEK CUT 2 — POMPON

FIG 5 — 1SQ = 2.5cm — BEAR EAR BEAR INNER EAR CUT 2 — POMPON — BEAR FRONT/BACK CUT 2 — BEAR NOSE AND MOUTH AREA CUT 1

# Brother & Sister Dolls

Sue & Sam are 42 cm tall.

## KNITTED DOLLS

The body, face and hair are knitted in one piece with a seam down the centre back. The neck is drawn in after the head has been filled. The legs, arms and clothes are knitted separately. The dolls are knitted in 5-ply yarn on finer needles than usual to give a firmer texture.

*Sue*
Use 25 g balls of yarn, quantities as follows—two light brown for skin, two blue for dress and one navy blue; small quantities orange, white, black yarn approximately 10 m 20-ply bouclé yarn for hair
two 8 mm shanked buttons for shoes
three 8 mm buttons for dress

*Sam*
Two light brown and two green 25 g balls yarn
small quantities of red, orange and black yarn
approximately 10 m bouclé yarn for hair
three 8 mm buttons
1 pr 2.75 (No. 12) knitting needles
one double-pointed needle
tapestry needle for sewing seams
polyester fibre for filling

*Abbreviations:* K—*knit*; P—*purl*; st(s)—*stitch(es)*; cont—*continue*; tog—*together*; st st—*stocking stitch*; inc—*increase* (knit into back of stitch to make extra stitch); dec—*decrease*; rep—*repeat*; alt—*alternate*; foll—*following*; beg—*beginning*; patt—*pattern*; pmon—*place marker on needle*; rem—*remaining*.

## Body

Cast on 64 sts in light brown. Work in st st for 12 cm ending with a purl row.
*Divide for armholes:* Knit 17, turn (*side back*). Work 10 rows st st ending knit row. Break off yarn. Join in yarn and knit 30 sts, turn (*front*). Work 10 rows st st ending knit row. Break off yarn. Join in yarn and knit rem 17 sts, turn

*Sue & Sam,
the Brother & Sister Dolls*

(*side back*). Work 10 rows st st ending knit row.
*Next row:* P16, P2 tog, P28, P2 tog, P16 (62 sts).
*Next row:* K15, K2 tog, K to last 17 sts K2 tog, K15.
*Next row:* P15, P2 tog, P to last 17 sts P2 tog, P15.
Rep previous 2 rows until 48 sts rem. Tie marker for neck. Work 10 rows st st ending purl row. Break off yarn.

## Hair

Take 3 m of bouclé yarn for separate ball for left side of hair.
*1st row:* Using bouclé yarn K14 (*right side head*), join in light brown, K20 (*face*), join in bouclé, K14 (*left side head*). Cont working with 3 separate balls, inc hair sections to top of face as follows:
*2nd row:* K15, P19, K14.
*3rd row:* K15, K18, K15.
*4th row:* K16, P17, K15.
*5th row:* K16, K16, K16.
*6th row:* K17, P15, K16.
*7th row:* K17, K14, K17.
*8th row:* K18, P13, K17.
*9th row:* K18, K12, K18.
Rep 9th row 3 times working face in st st. Break off light brown and knit 6 rows in bouclé.
*Next row:* K2 tog to end of row.
*Next row:* Knit. Rep these 2 rows until 6 sts rem. Cast off.

## Sue's leg

Cast on 30 sts in orange. St st 70 rows, alternating 2 rows each orange and white, ending with orange stripe.
*Next row:* Place first 11 sts on a holder. Join in white, K8, turn. Keeping stripe correct st st 11 rows, leave sts on needle.

## Shoe

In black, knit 11 sts from holder, pick up 11 sts along instep, K8 on needle. Using a double-pointed needle pick up 11 sts along instep, K rem 11 sts on needle (52 sts). Knit 8 rows garter st.
*1st shaping row:* (K2 tog, K23) twice, K2 tog (49 sts).
*2nd row:* K4, K2 tog, pmon, K13, pmon, K2 tog, K7, K2 tog, pmon, K13, pmon, K2 tog, K4 (45 sts).

*3rd row:* Knit.
*4th row:* Knit to within 2 sts of 1st marker, K2 tog, knit to 2nd marker, K2 tog, knit to within 2 sts of 3rd marker, K2 tog, knit to 4th marker, K2 tog, knit to end of row (41 sts). Rep 3rd and 4th rows twice (33 sts).
*Next row:* K2 tog, K12, K2 tog, K1, K2 tog, K12, K2 tog (29 sts).
*Next row:* K2 tog, K10, K2 tog, K1, K2 tog, K10, K2 tog. Cast off.

## Sam's leg

Cast on 30 sts in light brown, work in st st for 12 cm. Join in green, knit 4 rows. Join in red and work in rib of K2, P2 for 3 rows. Join in orange and cont in rib for 5 cm ending with right side facing. Join in black and knit 6 rows. Break off yarn.
*Next row:* Place first 11 sts on a holder. Join in black and knit 12 rows on next 8 sts. Leave sts on needle.
Follow directions for girl's shoe.

## Arm

Cast on 12 sts light brown. St st 16 rows inc first and last st in 3rd, 5th, 9th, 10th rows (20 sts), then dec first and last st in 15th and 16th rows (16 sts). Work 12 rows, inc first and last st in next row (18 sts). St st 27 rows. Cast off 2 sts at the beg of the next 4 rows. Cast off.

## Dress

**Back:** Cast on 64 sts in navy. Knit 6 rows. Join in blue, st st 10 cm ending knit row.
*Next row:* P2 tog across row (32 sts).
*Next row:* Join in navy blue K3, (P2, K2) 6 times, P2, K3.
*Next row:* P3, (K2, P2) 6 times, K2, P3*. Rep these 2 rows 16 times. Cast off 3 sts at beg of next 4 rows. Cast off.

**Front:** Work as for back to *, rep these 2 rows 3 times. Divide for placket opening.
*Next row:* Rib 17, cast on 1, turn.
*Next row:* K5, cont in rib to end of row. Working in rib with placket (3 sts) in garter st, work 28 rows, making buttonholes in 3rd, 15th, and 27th rows. (To make buttonhole knit to last 4 sts. K2, cast off 1st st, K2. Next row: K2, cast on 1, rib to end of row.)
*29th row:* Cast off 3 sts at beg of next and foll right side row for shoulder. Cast off rem sts. To complete other side: join in yarn at beg of placket and cast on 3 sts. Turn, work in rib with placket in garter st to match other side.

## Sam's Jumper

**Front:** Cast on 32 sts in green and work in rib for 6 cm. Foll directions for dress from placket opening.

**Back:** Cast on 32 sts and work in rib to match front at shoulders. Cast off 3 sts at beg of the next 4 rows. Cast off.

### Sleeve *(jumper and dress)*

Cast on 24 sts in navy/green, knit 6 rows. Join in blue/red, st st 20 rows inc first and last st in 1st, 9th and 17th rows. Cast off 3 sts at beg of next 4 rows. Cast off.

## Sam's shorts

Cast on 38 sts in red. Knit 6 rows, inc first and last st in alt rows (44 sts). Join in green, knit 4 rows. Cast off 3 sts at beg of the next 2 rows. Dec first and last st in alt rows until 30 sts rem. Knit 20 rows. Join in red, knit 6 rows. Cast off. Rep for other side.

## To make up

*Body:* Sew hair to face at sides on wrong side. Sew in yarn ends closing any holes around hairline. Using matching yarn run a gathering thread around hairline on wrong side. Pull up slightly to make hair fuller around face, secure ends well. Using matching colour run a gathering thread across body at neck marker on wrong side, leave ends unsecured on right side. Sew back body seam from top of head to base of body. Turn to right side. Fill head, pull up threads at neck and secure well. Fill remainder of body and sew across at base with seam at centre back.

*Leg:* Sew back seam of leg and foot. Turn to right side and fill. Fold in half at top with seam at centre back and sew across. Sew legs to body at base, leaving a small gap at centre.

*Arm:* Sew arm seam. Turn to right side and fill. Sew to body around armhole inserting more filling if necessary

before finishing seam.

*Foot strap:* Pick up 3 sts on inside of foot. Knit sufficient rows to cross foot. Cast off. Secure on other side, sew on button.

*Dress and jumper:* Sew placket extension across base on wrong side. Sew shoulder seams. Sew sleeve head to dress with shoulder seams at centre. Sew underarms and side seams. Sew on buttons.

*Collar:* Pick up 38 sts around neck and knit 6 rows. Cast off loosely.

*Belt:* Cast on 3 sts, knit 45 cm. Cast off. Sew in ends and tie around waist.

*Sam's shorts:* With right sides together, sew pieces together at centre front and back seams. Sew inner leg seam. Insert hat elastic around waist if necessary.

*Face:* Using 2 strands yarn, embroider eyes in satin stitch and mouth in backstitch. Make nose with concealed stitches in matching yarn.

# Rag Dolls

DESIGNED BY GWEN MERRILL

These lovely rag dolls are dramatic beauties — in shades of red, blue and white, with lacy trimmed dresses and long, beribboned pigtails.

*White haired doll*
40 × 90 cm wide plain navy blue cotton fabric for body
70 × 90 cm navy print cotton fabric for dress and pants
20 × 90 cm wide striped cotton fabric for legs
1 m each green ricrac braid, lace and green velvet ribbon
four 8 mm buttons
5 mm elastic
scraps white and red felt for eyes, nose and mouth
scrap red/white spot fabric for cheeks
22 m of 5-ply acrylic yarn for hair
approximately 500 g polyester fibre filling

*Yellow-haired doll*
40 × 90 cm wide calico for body
60 × 90 cm wide plain red cotton fabric for dress, panties and shoes
15 × 50 cm piece cotton ticking for apron
15 × 90 cm wide plain navy blue cotton for legs
navy blue bias binding
1.2 m ricrac braid
1 m each lace and navy blue ribbon
22 m, 5-ply acrylic yarn
scraps red and black felt for eyes and mouth
scrap red/white spot fabric for cheeks
four 8 mm buttons
5 mm elastic
approximately 500 g polyester fibre for filling

## To make patterns

Enlarge doll and dress patterns (*see Figs. 1 and 2, page 94*), following directions given on page 6, working to a scale of 1 sq = 2.5 cm. A 5 mm seam allowance is included on all pattern pieces.

*Rag Dolls*

## To make body

1. Cut four body pieces, four arms, two legs and two sole pieces. *Red shoes:* Cut leg pattern at line indicated, add 5 mm to each side for seams and cut in chosen fabrics. Cut 54, 36 cm lengths of yarn for hair; cut eyes, nose and mouth in felt. Add 3 mm to cheeks and cut two from spotted fabric.
2. Sew five lengths of hair to each side front between 5 mm seam allowance and mark A at top of head. Sew 22 lengths hair to each side head at back between 5 mm seam allowance and mark B.
3. With right side together sew centre front and back seams from top of head to crotch. Make sure that hair line is even on right side. Place front and back together with right side inside and sew from top of head to arm on both sides. Tie hair in bundles to keep it out of the way.
4. Sew around arms leaving top open. Clip thumb curve, trim and turn to right side. Fill arms to within 1 cm of raw edge and tack across to keep filling away from stitching line. With arm inside body and raw edges level sew from top of arm to legs. Clip neck curves and turn body to right side. Use a ruler to pack head and neck firmly with fibre. The doll's body does not need to be firmly filled.
5. Join shoe to leg if required. Fold leg with right side inside and sew front seam. Nick curve on front foot. Carefully make 3 mm nicks in seam allowance around lower edge of foot. With right sides together pin, matching centre back and front foot to same on sole. Sew, making sure nicks are confined to seam allowance. Trim seam and turn to right side. Fill feet and legs firmly with small pieces of fibre to within 1 cm of raw edges. Tack across with seam in middle of leg.
6. Turn seam allowance to inside around lower body. Insert legs and

stitch firmly to body on both sides.
7. Stitch or glue felt pieces to face. Turn in 3 mm on cheeks and tack around. Hem stitch to face. Arrange hair in bunches at side of head and secure with elastic bands and ribbons. Stitch to head with concealed stitches under bunches.

## Blue dress

1. Cut two yokes, two sleeves, one front on fold and two backs.
2. With right sides inside sew yokes together around neck edge and down back opening. Trim corners and nick neck edge. Turn to right side and then press.
3. With right sides together sew sleeves to back and front skirts. Press 2 cm to wrong side of back skirts and neaten raw edges. Gather up skirt including sleeves to fit yoke. With right sides together sew skirt to top yoke, with folded edge of back skirt matching edge of yoke. Fold under 5 mm on inside yoke and hem stitch over the raw edges.
4. Sew down underarm and side seams. Turn 5 mm then 3 cm to wrong side of bottom sleeve for casing. Make first stitching line at edge of hem leaving an opening for elastic, second line 1 cm from edge. Insert elastic and stitch securely.
5. Machine neaten and make a 1 cm hem on skirt. Sew lace to bottom of dress. Sew ricrac braid around neck and outer edge of yoke. Make buttonholes and sew on buttons.

## Red dress

1. Cut one front yoke on fold, two back yokes with extension, two 18 × 23 cm wide pieces for back skirt, one 18 × 40 cm wide piece for front skirt and two 27 × 18 cm wide pieces for sleeves.
2. With right sides together sew back yokes to front at shoulders. Gather front skirt and sew to front yoke at waist. Repeat for backs with no gathering from centre back to edge of the facing.
3. With right side facing sew sleeves to yokes from waistline across to other side, with fullness at shoulder. Sew down underarm and side seams.
4. Fold 5 mm then 2 cm to wrong side of bottom sleeve for casing. Make first stitching line at edge of hem leaving an opening for elastic, second line 1 cm from edge. Sew ricrac braid around edge of sleeve.

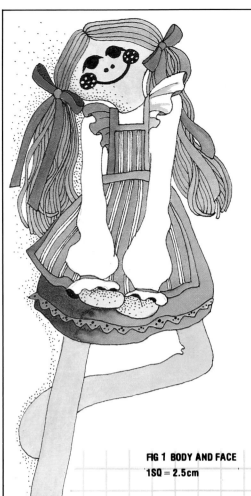

5. Machine neaten raw edges of back facings and fold at line indicated to right side of dress. Sew a length of bias binding around neck, with right side facing and ends overlapping back facings. Nick edge, turn binding and back facings to wrong side, press and slip hem.

6. Double machine neaten hem. Sew lace to bottom of dress and ricrac above lace. Make buttonholes, sew on buttons. Insert elastic in sleeves and sew securely.

## Apron

1. Cut one bib front and one 13 × 34 cm wide piece for skirt from ticking. Cut bias binding to measure as you sew.

2. Sew a length of binding with right side to wrong side of bib at top. Turn binding to right side, press and edge stitch binding on both sides.

3. Cut two 64 cm lengths binding for bib front sides and ties. Sew to wrong side of each side bib with ends extending at top. Fold extending ends in half with wrong side inside and edge stitch

along both sides to make neck ties. Turn binding to right side and edge stitch along each side.

4. Sew binding to sides and hem of skirt in same way. Gather skirt to 18 cm, mark centre and sew bib to skirt with wrong sides facing.

5. Cut a 122 cm length of binding for waist and ties. Mark centre and sew across wrong side of skirt and right side of bib front. Fold and sew ties as for neck. Press gathering flat, fold binding down and press. Edge stitch on both sides to match rest of apron.

## Pants (for both dolls)

1. Cut pants from chosen fabric. With right sides together, sew down centre back, centre front and leg seams.

2. Turn 5 mm then 1 cm to wrong side at waist for casing, sew leaving an opening to insert elastic. Turn 5 mm then 2 cm to wrong side on legs for casing. Sew first stitching line at edge of hem, leaving an opening for elastic, second line 1 cm from edge. Insert elastic and stitch securely.

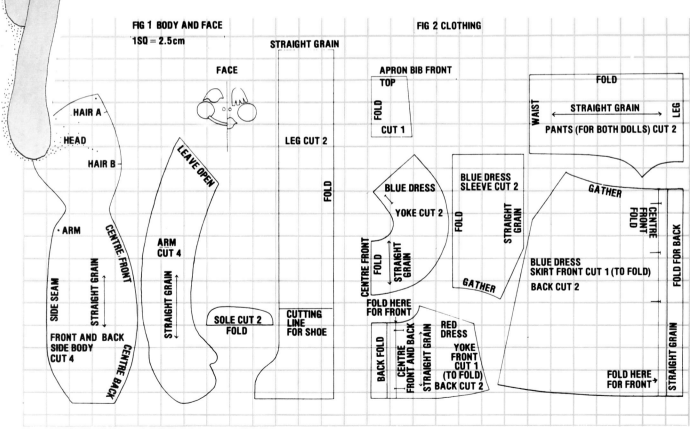

*Finger Puppets in Felt*

# Finger Puppets in Felt

DESIGNED BY PAMELA MANIKA

Make a tiny kingdom, with twelve separate figures. Decorate as colourfully as you like.

Assorted felt scraps
scraps of lace
white glue
tracing paper and stiff paper for
  patterns
ruler and pencil
black ball-point pen

Trace off and make basic pattern in stiff paper (*see Fig. 1, p. 96*). Following directions given on p. 6, draw up and trace off features and decorations for each puppet (*see Figs. 2-13, pp. 96-7*), working to a scale of 1 sq = 1 cm.

Cut basic pattern pieces in colours as indicated on diagrams (*see Figs. 2-13*).

## To assemble

Glue basic pattern pieces together by spreading glue approximately 5 mm around edge of puppet, leaving bottom opening free.

## Features and trimmings

Cut out features such as arms, eyes, hands, etc., for each puppet. Position them on basic puppet shape and glue in place. Fringe yellow felt to represent native's grass skirt and arm bands. Scraps of lace are used for dress of fairy and trimming for dress of princess. The witch's mouth and lines on king's robe are drawn with the pen.

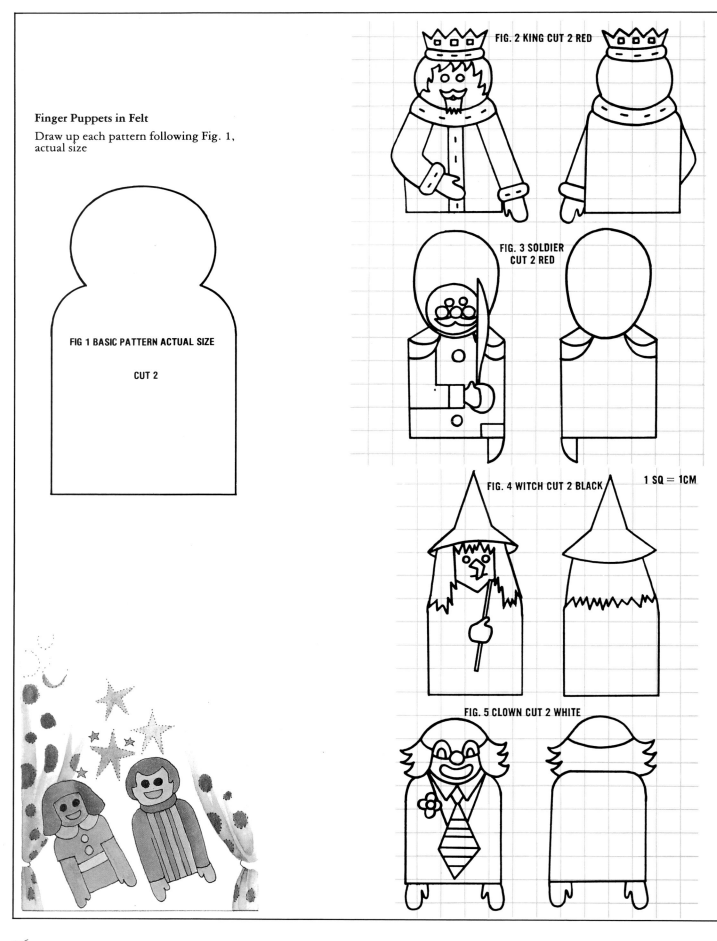

**Finger Puppets in Felt**

Draw up each pattern following Fig. 1, actual size

FIG 1 BASIC PATTERN ACTUAL SIZE

CUT 2

FIG. 2 KING CUT 2 RED

FIG. 3 SOLDIER CUT 2 RED

FIG. 4 WITCH CUT 2 BLACK

1 SQ = 1CM

FIG. 5 CLOWN CUT 2 WHITE

1 SQ = 1 CM

FIG. 6 FAIRY CUT 2 PINK

FIG. 8 GIRL CUT 2 YELLOW

FIG. 7 BOY CUT 2 BLUE

FIG. 9 WIZARD CUT 2 BLACK

FIG. 10 NATIVE CUT 2 BROWN

1 SQ = 1 CM

FIG. 12 FATHER CHRISTMAS CUT 2 RED

FIG. 11 PRINCESS CUT 2 PINK

FIG. 13 PIRATE CUT 2 GREEN

# Kindergarten Companions

DESIGNED BY GWEN MERRILL

Bright carry-bags and colourful dolls made from scraps for happy playground days!

## DOLLS
### (height 28 cm)

Scraps of calico and firm, non-fraying fabric
12-ply yarn
polyester fibre filling
tailor's chalk
hard pencil
sewing thread

Following directions on p. 6, enlarge pattern for doll (see Figs. 1 and 2, p. 101) working to a scale of 1 sq = 2.5 cm. Trace paper patterns for head and body and add a 5 mm seam allowance.

### How to appliqué

Firm tracing paper
chalk
sharp pencil
ruler
scissors

1. Make paper patterns of each shape and cut out. Mark outline on fabric in sharp pencil. Cut out leaving 5 mm around shape.
2. Mark position for appliqué on base fabric in chalk. Position appliqué pieces and press. Machine around shape on pencil line in small stitch.
3. Trim edges close to machining.
4. Adjust machine zigzag to widest setting and small close stitch. Loosen top tension of machine. The top satin stitch is pulled to wrong side by firmer lower tension, making stitch more even.
5. Zigzag around shape. Where colours overlap use straight stitch only.
6. To gain best results when appliqué-ing: for a firmer more even stitch, sew with paper underneath work and tear away from stitching on completion.

This also helps to feed the work evenly through the machine, especially when working around corners. Use iron-on interfacing to make fabrics firmer and a spray ironing aid on finished work. Protect work with fabric guard.

### Head (all dolls)

Cut two head sections in calico. Appliqué eyes, cheeks and mouth as shown in Fig. 1.

**Hair** (see Fig. 3, p. 101): Working on the right side of face between marks, make 3 cm loops in yarn close together with one folded edge level with raw edge, loops lying on face. Sew 5 mm from edge making loops as you go. Sew two layers on back head in same way.

### Overalls doll (see Fig. 1)

Cut two body sections in material for overalls. Make a paper pattern for front and back of overalls (do not add seam allowance). Mark outline of overalls on to body in hard pencil or chalk, do not cut out. Cut two body sections, ending 1 cm below waistline of overalls, for shirt. Place shirt underneath, right side facing wrong side of overalls, raw edges together. Machine sew outline of overalls on front and back. Cut away excess fabric close to machining. Appliqué raw edges of overalls. Appliqué heart motif on front in same way. Sew feet to legs. Press and make up following directions for Heart motif doll.

### Heart motif doll (see Fig. 2)

Cut two body sections. Appliqué heart motif to front body. Sew face and back head to body sections at neck. With right sides together and hair inside sew around head and body twice using small machine stitch, leaving opening at side. Clip into corners, trim seam allowance on curves. Turn to right side. Fill and stitch opening securely.

### Patchwork doll (see Fig. 2)

Cut body pattern into sections as marked, note straight grain on each piece. Add 5 mm seam allowance and cut four each arms, legs, feet, upper and lower body in different fabrics. Remember to reverse pattern for left and right side of body. Sew pieces with right sides together to make front and back body. Press seams and make up following directions for Heart motif doll.

## HOUSE BAG
### (36 × 30 × 8 cm)

40 × 115 cm wide denim
20 × 90 cm wide red fabric
two 20 × 40 cm pieces of thick wool for padding roof
scraps yellow, green and red spotted fabric
matching thread
two 16 × 1.5 cm strips plastic cut from ice cream container to stiffen roof between handles

1. Following directions on p. 6, enlarge pattern for bag and appliqué design (see Fig. 4, p. 101). Seam allowances included on pattern are 5 mm unless otherwise indicated.
2. Cut in denim: two pieces for front and back the complete shape of bag, one 31 cm × 9 cm wide piece for base; two 34 cm × 8 cm wide pieces for handles; two 23 cm × 5 cm wide pieces to cover side seam which is on right side of bag. In red, cut two roof sections adding 3 cm extra at lower edge for hem. Cut two roof sections in thick material without hem. Make paper patterns for each part of appliqué design, mark outline in sharp pencil on selected fabrics and cut out 5 mm from outline. *Note:* Cut grass and door to bottom of bag.
3. Mark position of appliqué in chalk on front of bag (see Fig. 1), for placement measurements. Place appliqué pieces in position, press and sew following directions for Appliqué.
4. Handles: Turn in 1 cm on both sides

of handle. Press folded edges in to meet at centre. Topstitch evenly with four rows machining. Baste handles to top of bag at position marked with wrong sides facing and handles pointing down.

5. With right side of roof facing *wrong side of bag*, baste roof and padding across top of bag covering handles. Sew roof to bag across top from A to A. Secure handles with extra row of machining. Clip corners, turn roof on to right side and press. Make back of bag in same way.

6. Sew side seams with *wrong sides together* and roof extended. Press seams open on right side. Prepare strips to cover seams. Turn in 1 cm on both sides of strip. Place over seams with ends under roof line and topstitch to match handles. Fold down roof, turn under 3 cm hem and press. Insert plastic strips at top of roof between handles. Baste roof to bag at hem. Topstitch around roof 2 cm from top edges and hem.

7. Turn bag to wrong side, clip at corners, sew to base. Zigzag seams. Turn to right side and press.

## BED BAG
### (41 × 30 cm wide)

40 × 115 cm wide denim
30 × 90 cm wide firm red fabric

scraps of fabric for patchwork and pillow
red and navy sewing thread
15 × 23 cm piece thick material for padding pillow
iron-on interfacing if required
Cut out in denim: one 96 × 34 cm piece, two 34 × 8 cm pieces for bag and handles; in red, one 49 × 25 cm, one 15 × 23 cm piece for pocket and pillow; in navy, one 13 × 19 cm piece for pillow; for patchwork 25, 5 cm squares in different fabrics.
*Note:* 5 mm seam allowances are included on all pieces except where otherwise indicated.

### Pillow

1. Mark position for pillow in chalk, 8 cm from top at centre, to measure 14 × 22 cm wide (*see Fig. 5*) for appliqué positions. Appliqué red pillow to bag with padding underneath at position marked following directions for appliqué on page 102. Sew navy section on top to leave, when finished, a 2 cm border of red at top and sides only.

### Quilt Pocket

With right sides facing, sew patchwork pieces together to form a 21 cm square. Press. Fold red pocket piece in half and press centre fold. Open out. Appliqué patchwork square to one side 2 cm from fold and 2.5 cm from remaining raw edges to make a square 20 cm. Fold pocket in half and position with top folded edge to overlap bottom edge of pillow by 1 cm. Appliqué 5 mm from raw edges with base of pocket flat on bag and slanting sides in to match pillow edge at top to allow for doll. Using a straight stitch, sew pocket to bag again around sides and lower edge of patchwork next to satin stitch.

### Handles

Turn in 1 cm on both sides of handle. Press folded edges in to meet at centre. Topstitch evenly with four rows machining. Trim both handles to match and zigzag raw ends.

### Bag

Neaten sides using zigzag. Fold bag in half, right sides together, and sew side seam. Press seam open. To form base: fold corner of bag to form a triangle, with open side seam in the centre (*see Fig. 6*). Stitch diagonally across corner 1.5 cm from point of triangle. Turn bag to right side. Turn in 2.5 cm twice at

top of bag for hem. Baste handles inside bag with ends level with lower edge of hem, 7.5 cm from side seam. Topstitch hem at top of bag and lower edge securing handles. Sew an X on the handles to reinforce.

## ROCKET BAG
### (41 × 30 cm wide)

40 × 115 cm wide denim
scraps coloured fabric
navy thread for bag and handles
1. Cut one 96 × 34 cm piece, two 34 × 8 cm wide pieces in denim for bag and handles. Following directions on p. 101, enlarge appliqué design (*see Fig. 8*).
2. Following instructions for appliqué cut rocket shape in green and position on bag 8 cm from top with wing 6.5 cm from side. Outline stitch only. Add stripes, wings, nose, tail sections and trim before working satin stitch over entire design in navy. Position numbers beside rocket 6.5 cm from side and appliqué. Make up bag following instructions for Bed bag.

## SKATEBOARD BAG
### (41 × 30 cm wide)

40 × 115 cm wide denim
scraps coloured fabric
red thread
1. Cut one 96 × 34 cm piece, two 34 × 8 cm wide pieces in denim for bag and handles. Following directions on p. 101, enlarge appliqué design (*see Fig. 8*).
2. Following instructions for appliqué cut out all pieces.
3. Outline stitch in the following order: top body—leaving arm covering skateboard unstitched, face, helmet, shoes, pants. Cut inside of unstitched arm to insert skateboard. Sew skateboard with hand and arm on top. Add stripes, patches and face. Appliqué in widest stitch around all sections. Make up bag following instructions for Bed bag.

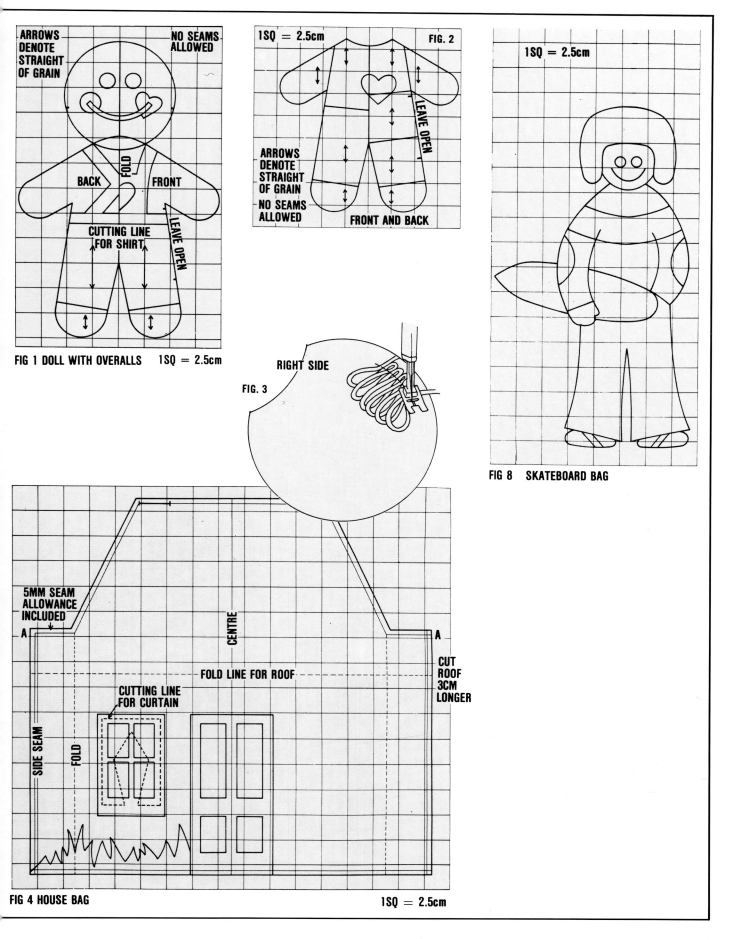

ARROWS DENOTE STRAIGHT OF GRAIN

NO SEAMS ALLOWED

BACK

FOLD

FRONT

CUTTING LINE FOR SHIRT

LEAVE OPEN

**FIG 1 DOLL WITH OVERALLS**     1SQ = 2.5cm

1SQ = 2.5cm     FIG. 2

ARROWS DENOTE STRAIGHT OF GRAIN

NO SEAMS ALLOWED

LEAVE OPEN

**FRONT AND BACK**

1SQ = 2.5cm

**FIG 8    SKATEBOARD BAG**

RIGHT SIDE

FIG. 3

5MM SEAM ALLOWANCE INCLUDED

A

CENTRE

FOLD LINE FOR ROOF

A

CUT ROOF 3CM LONGER

CUTTING LINE FOR CURTAIN

SIDE SEAM

FOLD

**FIG 4 HOUSE BAG**     1SQ = 2.5cm

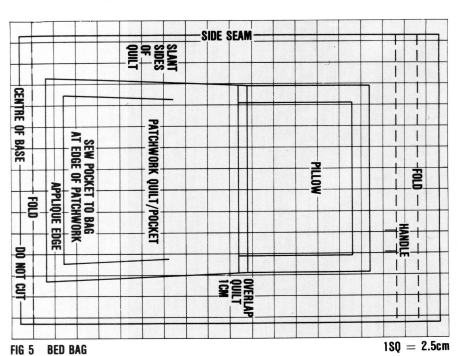

FIG 5    BED BAG

1SQ = 2.5cm

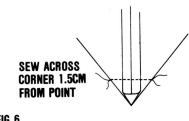

**SEW ACROSS CORNER 1.5CM FROM POINT**

FIG 6

FIG 7    ROCKET BAG          1SQ = 2.5cm

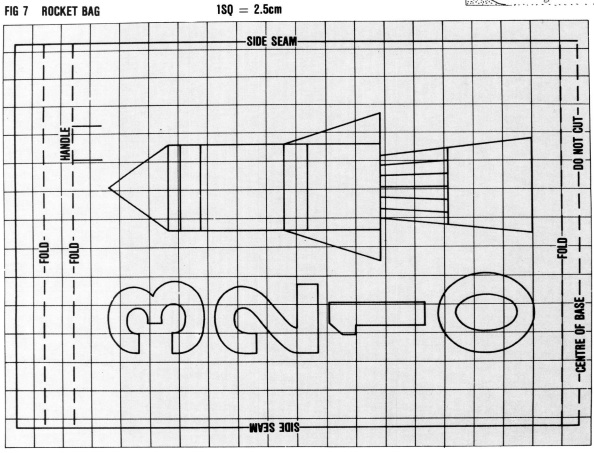

# Knit a Baby Bear

(PHOTOGRAPHED SECOND FROM RIGHT ON THE FRONT COVER)

## He is 24 cm tall, dressed for play.

Legs, body and head are knitted in one piece. Arms and ears are knitted separately. Knitted in 8 ply yarn on 3 mm (No. 11) needles to give a firmer texture.

One ball each brown and light blue yarn (25 g balls)
small quantities red, white, green, black and beige yarn for bag
1 pr 10 mm plastic animal eyes
two 4 mm buttons
1 pr 2.75 mm (No. 12) knitting needles
Polyester fibre filling
1 pr 3 mm (No. 11) knitting needles
tapestry needle for sewing seams

*Abbreviations*: K — *knit*; P — *purl*; st (s) — *stitch(es)*; pr — *pair*; cont — *continue*; st st — *stocking stitch*; tog — *together*; alt — *alternate*; dec — *decrease*; inc — *increase*; rep — *repeat*.

*Tension:* 5 sts (st st) = 2 cm, 7 rows (st st) = 2 cm.

*Legs* (work 2): Cast on in red 27 sts, Knit 16 rows.

*Top of shoe* (first leg): * K15, cast off 7 sts, K5 *. Knit 2 rows on these 20 sts.

*Cuff:* Knit 2 rows each green, white, green. Change to blue and st st 8 rows. Place sts on holder. Rep for second leg working top of shoe from * to * in reverse.

*Next row:* Knit across both legs 40 sts. Cont in st st for 17 rows. Knit 3 rows. Break off yarn.

*Jumper:* Work 15 rows st st, one white, one green row.

*Shape shoulders:* K9, K2 tog, K18, K2 tog, K9, 38 sts.

*Next and alt rows:* Purl.

*Next row:* K9, K2 tog, K16, K2 tog, K9, 36 sts. Cont to dec in same manner until 32 sts rem. Purl one row.

*Next row:* K9, K2 tog, K4, K2 tog, K4, K2 tog, K9, 29 sts.

*Head:* Change to brown and purl one row.

*Next row:* K9, inc once in next st, K4, K 3 times in next st, K4, inc once in next st, K9, 33 sts.

*Next and alt rows:* Purl.

*Next row:* K9, inc once in next st, K6, K 3 times in next st, K6 inc once in next st, K9, 37 sts. Cont to inc in same manner at sides of head and for snout until 45 sts. St st 5 rows.

*Next row:* K20, cast off 5, K20, 40 sts. St st 7 rows without shaping.

*Next row:* K8, K2 tog, K8, K2 tog twice, K8, K2 tog, K8, 36 sts.

*Next and alt rows:* Purl.

*Next row:* K8, K2 tog, K6, K2 tog twice, K6, K2 tog, K8, 32 sts. Cont to dec in same manner until 28 sts rem. Purl one row. Cast off.

*Arms* (work 2): Cast on 11 sts. Purl one row.

*Next row:* * K1, inc once in next st *, rep from * to * across row 16 sts. Work in st st for 5 rows, then 16 rows in stripes to match jumper. Cast off.

*Ears* (work 4): Cast on 11 sts in brown. St st 3 rows. Dec both ends of row in next and foll knit rows until 5 sts rem. Cast off.

## To make up

Using brown, weave across neck on wrong side leaving ends on right side for pulling in neck. In matching yarn sew tops of shoe and snout openings. With right sides tog sew side of shoe then sole, noting that seam is on inside leg. Sew each leg, then cont sewing up back seam to top of head. Fasten off all threads securely. Turn to right side and fill through top opening, defining features with small pieces of fibre. Fill neck and head firmly, push out snout. Attach plastic eyes before sewing across top of head. Press ears flat on wrong side under cloth. With right sides tog sew around by machine in matching thread, leaving straight side open. Turn to right side. Sew to sides

of head over corners of top seam. Make a tiny tuck in centre of front ear. Embroider nose and mouth in black. With right sides inside sew up arms. Turn to right side and fill. Sew to body and shoulder. Press seam flat. Sew buttons at centre front. Pull in neck and secure threads.

*Braces:* Pick up 3 sts at side front waist and knit length required to cross at back. Cast off and sew ends at back waist. Sew buttons at front.

*Scarf:* Using 2.75 mm needles, cast on 4 sts and work in garter st for 30 cm. Fasten off.

# Teddy Bears' Picnic

This quilt, the pillow sham and Teddy toys are all designed to bring pleasure to little people.

*For quilt, sham, cushion and two bears*
115 cm wide cotton or polyester cotton blend fabric
2.7 m pre-quilted striped or print fabric
2.7 m yellow small print or spot fabric
3.7 m green small print or spot fabric
30 cm interfacing
1.4 m white lining fabric
polyester fibre filling for dolls
one 30 cm square made or purchased cushion insert
one bed pillow for sham
green and yellow thread
quantity yellow yarn to tie quilt
dressmaker's carbon
tracing wheel, ruler
lightweight cardboard
large-eyed needle

*Note:* Check size of pillow to be used and adjust size of sham if necessary before cutting. See directions below for making cushion insert.

Actual size appliqué patterns are on p. 106 Trace bear on folded tracing paper; turn paper over to copy on blank half, then open it for full pattern. Trace vest and collar on folded paper the same way. Trace all inside design lines on to fabric bear and bow pieces, using dressmaker's carbon and wheel. Use the photograph for the direction of the stripes when cutting and positioning bear motifs. Use yellow thread for seaming throughout and 12 mm seam allowance except where otherwise indicated.

*Cutting:* Draw, cut and label the following pieces.

## QUILT
### (100 × 132 cm)

*From quilted fabric:* Twelve 33 cm squares, two 7.5 × 125 cm side borders, two 7.5 × 105 cm top and bottom borders. *From green spot:* One 105 × 135 cm quilt backing, forty-eight 4.5 × 33 cm border stripes, six vests and bows. *From yellow spot and white lining:* Twelve bears each. *From unquilted fabric:* Remove quilting and padding from scraps of quilted fabric. Press scraps and cut 12 collar halves.
*Note:* In half the blocks the bear is wearing a collar and vest and in remaining ones only the bow.

## CUSHION
### (30.5 cm square)

*Cushion top:* Follow measurements and cutting directions as for a quilted square. *From green spot:* Two 10 × 152 cm ruffle strips. *From yellow spot:* Two 7.5 × 152 cm ruffle strips, one 20.5 × 34 cm back and one 25.5 × 34 cm back (*they will overlap*).

## PILLOW SHAM
### (45 × 61 cm)

*From quilted fabric:* One 48 × 63.5 cm top piece. *From green spot:* Two 7 × 48 cm and two 7 × 63.5 cm border strips, one vest, one bow and three 12.5 × 193 cm ruffle strips. *From yellow spot:* Three 10 × 193 cm ruffle strips, one 48 × 49.5 cm and one 33 × 49.5 cm sham back pieces, two bears. *From white lining:* Two bears. *From unquilted fabric:* Prepare fabric as for quilt above and cut collar halves.

## TWO STUFFED BEARS
### (height 24 cms)

Add 12 mm seam allowance all around when cutting bear patterns from fabric; also at shoulders and sides of vest and at shoulders of bow and collar. *From yellow:* Four bears. *From interfacing:* Two bears. *From green spot:* One bow and one vest. *From unquilted stripe:* Two collar halves as for quilt above.

### To make quilt

1. *Making quilt squares:* Turn under and press 6 mm on one long edge of each border strip for squares. With raw edges of stripes matching raw edges of square, pin and edgestitch left and right borders to square, then stitch top and bottom strips to square the same way.
2. With lining between, pin and baste a bear appliqué to the centre of each square. Baste bows or vests and collars on bear (*see photograph*).
3. With machine set on widest zigzag satin stitch and green thread, stitch around edges of bear, vest and collar or bow, fill in eyes and nose. Use a narrower stitch for mouth. Straight stitch over remaining lines with same colour thread. Press each square.
4. *Assembling quilt top:* Arrange squares as shown in photograph. Working across quilt from left to right, pin and stitch three squares together, using 12 mm seams. Complete four rows this way, then stitch rows together to form quilt top.
5. Pin and stitch left and right borders to quilt, right sides together and edges matching. Press. Stitch top and bottom borders in same way.
6. With right sides together and edges matching, pin, then stitch quilt to backing, rounding corners slightly and leaving a 50 cm opening at bottom. Turn to right side; pin and topstitch opening closed.
7. With yarn in needle, make a stitch through all layers at each corner of squares. Tie a knot on quilt side.

### To make cushion and sham

1. Prepare and stitch cushion and sham top following photograph and Steps 1, 2 and 3 for quilt squares.
2. Taking up 6 mm, seam two short ends of green ruffle strips together, making one long strip, press. Stitch a 6 mm double-turned hem along one edge. Stitch gathering line 12 mm from raw edge. Stitch ends together to form a circle. Pull up gathering approximately 15 cm larger than top. Assemble a yellow ruffle same way. Distribute gathering evenly.
3. Pin yellow ruffle around top, with right sides together and edges matching, taking tucks at corners. Stitch 12 mm from edge. Pin and stitch green ruffle over yellow in same way.

*Teddy Bears' Picnic — quilt, pillow sham and bears*

4. *Back:* Stitch a 6 mm double-turned hem across one long edge of each piece. With ruffles inward, place slightly larger piece on front, right sides together and raw edges even. Place the second piece on opposite end, lapping back pieces at centre. Baste all around, 12 mm from edges. Stitch all layers together just inside ruffle stitching. Clip in diagonally at corners close to the stitching. Turn to right side; press. Place cushion insert or pillow inside.

*Cushion insert:* Cut two pieces of calico or lining fabric same size as quilt square. Place together and taking a 12 mm seam stitch, leave an opening on one side. Turn through and stuff firmly. Sew across opening.

BEAR QUILT APPLIQUE PATTERNS

BOW (ACTUAL SIZE)

BEAR (ACTUAL SIZE, ½ PATTERN)

STRIPED FABRIC

SPOT FABRIC

PLACE ON FOLD

## To make bears

1. Pin interfacing to wrong side of two bears.

2. Follow quilt directions for placement of clothes and stitching features on bears. Bring all stitching on clothes beyond 6 mm seamline.

3. Right sides together, stitch fronts to backs using 6 mm seam and leaving opening on leg for turning. Clip curves and into corners.

4. Turn to right side and press, stuff. Handstitch opening closed.

*Dolls to Learn From*

# Dolls to Learn From

DESIGNED BY GWEN MERRILL

Simon and Sally are made to be dressed and undressed over and over again!
Little fingers learn, through playing with these dolls, to put clothes on in the right order,
do up and undo buttons and zips, and fasten the laces and buttons on shoes.

## BOY AND GIRL DOLLS
### *(height 42 cm)*

*For both dolls*
50 × 150 cm wide one-way stretch
fabric
approximately 500 g polyester fibre
filling
15 × 90 cm tan felt for hair

scraps red and black felt for eyes and
mouth
*Sally's clothing*
30 × 90 cm wide check cotton fabric for
blouse and pants
30 × 50 cm wide piece blue corduroy
for pinafore
scrap white cotton fabric for collar
one 10 cm nylon zip
scrap leather or vinyl for shoes
three 8 mm red buttons for blouse

two 15 mm red buttons for pinafore
two 10 mm shanked buttons for shoes
length 5 mm elastic
40 cm blue bias binding
sewing threads to match
*Simon's clothing*
20 × 90 cm wide striped cotton for shirt
30 × 45 cm wide piece blue corduroy
for trousers
scrap white cotton fabric for collar
one 10 cm red nylon zip

scrap leather or vinyl for boots and
  braces
four 15 mm blue buttons for trousers
two 8 mm red buttons for shirt
1 m fine cord
sewing threads to match
*Note:* A polyester thread and ballpoint
machine needle are advised, to stitch
knit fabric. It makes for stronger seams
and also avoids making holes in fabric.
Use a heavy cotton thread (36) for
stitching shoes and boots. Use a nylon
zip only in clothing.

## To make patterns

Enlarge doll and clothing patterns (*see
Figs. 1 and 2, page 109*) following directions given on page 6, **working to a
scale of 1 sq = 2.5 cm.** A 5 mm seam
allowance is included on doll body and
clothing patterns. A 2 mm allowance is
included for shoes and hair.

## To make dolls

1. Fold fabric with right side inside.
Cut two body pieces and mark neck
dart on wrong side of both pieces, ankle
dart on front foot only. Cut hair tufts,
back and front hair pieces, eyes and
mouth from felt.

2. Tack hair piece on right side of front
and back head, stitch in matching
thread 2 mm from edge. Stitch eyes and
mouth the same way. Pleat tufts and
stitch to top of front head with tufts
facing down towards face.

3. Fold body pieces along centre of
darts with right side inside and stitch
curve, leaving 5 mm at side seams.
With right sides together stitch twice
around body pieces, leaving an opening
for filling. Stretch fabric slightly as you
sew. Clip curves and trim seams where
necessary. Turn to right side.

4. Insert small pieces of filling in arms,
legs and ears to lines indicated, stitch
across. Fill body and head, top stitch
across opening.

## Sally's clothing

**Blouse:** 1. Cut one back, two fronts
and two collars. With right sides together sew fronts to back at shoulder/
sleeve seams and neaten. Sew around
outer edge of collar pieces with right
sides inside. Trim seams and turn to
right side. Press the seams and the
collar.

2. Pin collar to right side of neck edge
with all raw edges together, matching
centre fronts with edge of collar.
Machine neaten edge of facings at front
and fold back on to right side of

garment overlapping collar. Sew round
neck from folded edge of facing to
other side. Zigzag seam and stretch as
you sew. Turn facing to wrong side and
edge stitch neck seam to garment from
right side underneath collar only.

3. Double machine neaten across edge
of sleeve. Fold garment with right side
inside, sew and neaten underarm and
down side seam. Double machine
neaten lower edge of garment.

4. Make buttonholes on correct side
and sew on buttons.

**Pinafore:** 1. Cut one back and one
front with pile running the same way
and two straps 14 × 4 cm wide.

2. Cut down centre front to dot and
diagonally across two cords to create V
piece. Make opening for zip by pressing
these edges to wrong side. Pin zip with
top 15 mm from raw edge. Edge stitch
on right side, down sides and carefully
across zip at bottom.

3. With right side inside sew and
neaten side seams. Sew matching bias
binding on right side, from side of bib
front across back to other side. Nick
seam, turn to wrong side and press.
Top stitch 5 mm from edge on right
side. Zigzag across raw edges on front.
Fold material above top of zip to wrong
side and stitch across from right side on
both sides.

4. To make straps, zigzag down one
long side of each strap. Press raw edge
15 mm on wrong side. Press neatened
edge over raw edge. Stitch down centre
of strap through the three layers. Zigzag
across raw ends of each strap. Sew
straps to wrong side of back on an
angle to cross over. Make buttonholes
on front. Dress doll and mark position
of buttons on strap.

**Pants:** 1. Cut two pieces. Sew and
neaten centre back and front seams,
then leg seam. Turn 5 mm then 10 mm
to wrong side at waist for casing and
sew leaving an opening for elastic.
Turn 5 mm then 20 mm to wrong side
of leg edges for casing and frill. Sew
first stitching line at edge of hem,
second line 1 cm from edge. Leave
opening for elastic. Measure elastic to
fit legs and waist and insert.

## Simon's clothing

**Shirt:** Make following directions given
above for the girl's blouse.

**Trousers:** 1. Cut one back and one
front with pile running the same way.

2. Insert zip as directed for girl's pinafore above.

3. With right sides together sew and

neaten side seams and inside leg seam
making a wide curve at the crotch. Nick
curve and turn trousers to right side.
Zigzag raw edges of legs and waist.
Turn corduroy to wrong side at waist,
level with top of zip and top stitch 1 cm
from edge on right side.

4. Turn 1 cm to wrong side on each leg
and hem. Sew buttons on right side of
front and wrong side of back for braces.
Cut braces in leather. Cut buttonhole as
marked on front first, with razor blade.
Fit on doll to cross at back and mark
the position for the back buttonhole.

**Shoes:** 1. *To machine stitch shoes:* Practise sewing leather before you begin.
Use a heavier thread and larger stitch
than for garments. Adjust the tension
and use slowest speed on your machine.
Sew with paper underneath leather to
ease it through machine. Practise sewing a straight piece of leather to a curve,
keeping stitches 2 mm from edge.

2. *To hand stitch shoes:* First machine
with large stitches around sole and shoe
separately, 2 mm from edge, without
thread in needle. Carefully line up holes
and backstitch shoe to sole from the top
side.

*Girl's shoes:* 1. Cut a pair of shoes and
two soles. Starting from back, stitch
around top of shoe including strap 2
mm from the edge. With wrong sides
together stitch back seam 2 mm from
edge. Do not reverse stitching. Take
threads to inside of seam and tie off.

2. Mark centre front on right side of
shoe with a small dot and centre front
and back on wrong side of sole. With
centre backs matching and wrong sides
together, stitch shoe to sole curving
shoe as you sew. If top shoe tends to
move too much, use tip of scissors to
hold in place and push under foot as
you sew. Take threads to inside and tie
off. Cut buttonholes and sew on buttons. Trim seam if necesssary.

*Boy's boots:* 1. Cut two boots and two
soles. Starting from the back, stitch
around top of shoes including tongue, 2
mm from edge and on lines indicated
on pattern. Tie ends on wrong side.

2. Mark centre front on right side of
boot and wrong side of sole. With
wrong sides together stitch on top side
from top of boot at back, matching
centre fronts as you sew around to back
on other side. Curve top to sole as you
sew. Take threads to inside and tie off.
Pierce holes as marked on pattern and
insert cord for laces. Trim boot if
necessary.

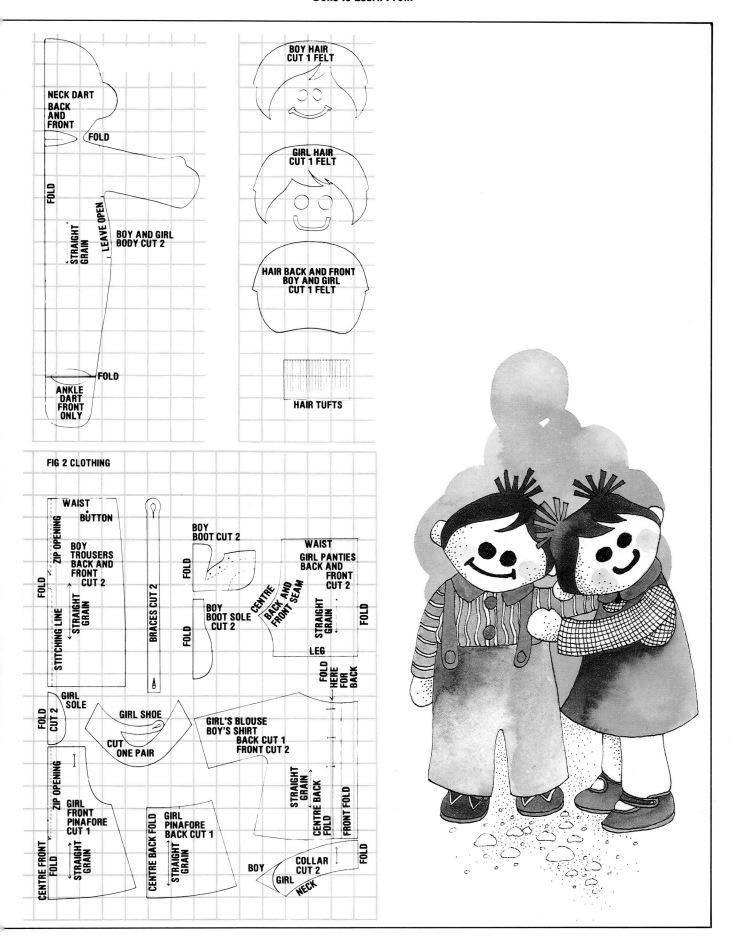

NECK DART
BACK
AND
FRONT

FOLD

FOLD

LEAVE OPEN

STRAIGHT GRAIN

BOY AND GIRL
BODY CUT 2

FOLD

ANKLE
DART
FRONT
ONLY

BOY HAIR
CUT 1 FELT

GIRL HAIR
CUT 1 FELT

HAIR BACK AND FRONT
BOY AND GIRL
CUT 1 FELT

HAIR TUFTS

**FIG 2 CLOTHING**

WAIST

BUTTON

ZIP OPENING

FOLD

BOY
TROUSERS
BACK AND
FRONT
CUT 2

STITCHING LINE

STRAIGHT GRAIN

BRACES CUT 2

BOY
BOOT CUT 2

FOLD

FOLD

BOY
BOOT SOLE
CUT 2

CENTRE BACK AND FRONT SEAM

WAIST

GIRL PANTIES
BACK AND
FRONT
CUT 2

STRAIGHT GRAIN

FOLD

LEG

FOLD HERE FOR BACK

GIRL
SOLE
CUT 2

FOLD

GIRL SHOE

CUT
ONE PAIR

GIRL'S BLOUSE
BOY'S SHIRT
BACK CUT 1
FRONT CUT 2

STRAIGHT GRAIN

CENTRE BACK FOLD

FRONT FOLD

FOLD

ZIP OPENING

GIRL
FRONT
PINAFORE
CUT 1

STRAIGHT GRAIN

CENTRE FRONT FOLD

CENTRE BACK FOLD

GIRL
PINAFORE
BACK CUT 1

STRAIGHT GRAIN

BOY

GIRL

COLLAR
CUT 2

NECK

FOLD

# Index

Published by **Murdoch Books**®, a division of Murdoch Magazines Pty Ltd,
213 Miller Street, North Sydney NSW 2060

Editors: Margaret Olds,
    Ingaret Ward, Joy Hayes
Designer: Dawn Daly
Doll and toy illustrations:
    Dee Huxley
Photography:
    Andy Payne, Tom Berry

Publisher: Anne Wilson
Publishing Manager: Catie Ziller
Managing Editor: Susan Tomnay
Art Director: Lena Lowe
International Manager:
    Mark Newman
Marketing Manager: Mark Smith
National Sales Manager:
    Keith Watson
Key Accounts Sales Manager:
    Kim Deacon
Photo Librarian: Dianne Bedford

National Library of Australia
Cataloguing-in-Publication Data
Treasury of dolls and cuddly toys
ISBN 0 86411 142 8.
Includes index.
1. Title. 1. Dollmaking.
2. Soft toy making.
(Series: Family Circle
Homemaker Library)
745.59221

Printed by Prestige Litho, Qld
Typeset by Savage Type Pty Ltd,
Brisbane

First printed 1983
Reprinted 1984, 1986, 1990, 1995
© Text, design, photography and
illustrations Murdoch Books® 1990

Murdoch Books® is a trade mark of
Murdoch Magazines Pty Ltd.

Australian distribution to
supermarkets and newsagents by
Gordon & Gotch Ltd,
68 Kingsgrove Road,
Belmore NSW 2192